MIND BODY POWER

THE SELF-HELP BOOK ON ACCELERATED LEARNING

To Kevin
Warm wishes
Moni Storz

MIND
BODY
POWER

THE SELF-HELP BOOK
ON ACCELERATED
LEARNING

Moni Lai Storz

TIMES BOOKS INTERNATIONAL
Singapore • Kuala Lumpur

© 1989 Moni Lai Storz

Illustrations by Chen Nen Seh

Published by Times Books International
an imprint of Times Editions Pte Ltd
Times Centre
1 New Industrial Road
Singapore 536196

Times Subang
Lot 46, Subang Hi-Tech Industrial Park
Batu Tiga
40000 Shah Alam
Selangor Darul Ehsan
Malaysia

Reprinted 1990, 1993, 1995

All rights reserved. No part of this publication may be reproduced
or transmitted in any form or by any means, electronic or mechanical,
including photocopying, recording or any information storage or
retrieval system, without written permission from the publisher.

Printed in Singapore

ISBN 981 204 137 0

For my parents

Contents

About the Author	ix
Acknowledgements	xi
Introduction	xii
1 Your Mind's Potential and Power	1
2 What is Accelerative Learning?	6
3 Relaxation	19
4 Creative Visualisation	40
5 Accelerative Learning Programmes	50
6 Teaching Others — You as Teacher	68
7 New Discoveries	88
Appendix	91
References	94
Index	95

About the author

Dr Moni Lai Storz is a senior lecturer in the School of Social and Behavioural Studies at Chisholm Institute of Technology, Melbourne, Australia. She holds a doctoral degree in sociology from Monash University (Melbourne, Australia).

During the many years that she has been teaching, Dr Storz has gained extensive research experience in Asia and Australia. She has drawn on this to design and develop programmes in Australia and overseas for both the private and public sectors. As an education and management consultant to industry and government bodies, Dr Storz specialises in stress management, time management, cross-cultural communication and negotiation skills. Her training methodology is based on the principles of accelerative learning and teaching.

Dr Storz is a member of the Sociological Association of Australia and New Zealand (SAANZ), member of the Accelerative Learning Society of Australia (ALSA) and member of the Australian Institute of Training and Development (AITD).

Acknowledgements

To write any book requires the help and support of many people. I wish to thank Ian Lewis for introducing me to accelerative learning and teaching. My own learning and teaching have never been the same since.

Shirley Hew of Times Books International asked me to write this book, and I must thank her for making several weeks of my life hysterically busy.

Dr Naomi White, friend and colleague, read the first draft of the book. For her support and friendship through the trials and tribulations of a writer's life, I am always grateful.

Evelyn Low, Director of Tadika Krisaliz in Kuala Lumpur, was kind enough to invite me to be the education consultant for her kindergarten after listening to my ideas on accelerative learning. I am proud to be associated with Tadika Krisaliz as the first kindergarten in Malaysia to use accelerative learning principles for preschoolers. For her faith in me and her assistance in implementing my theoretical ideas, I am grateful.

To all my other friends and family members who are ever ready to listen to my ideas on accelerative learning and teaching, I thank them with love.

Introduction

This book is written for anyone who believes that learning is his or her natural birthright. Essentially this book is about how to learn. Once you have mastered the method of how to learn, then you can learn anything. Everything is possible.

There is no such being as the person who cannot learn. Even a mentally retarded and physically retarded child has some ability to learn. There is only the person who is unable to teach. Or one who teaches badly and destructively.

Everyone of us starts to learn the minute that we are born. I see learning simply as the process whereby the human being acquires new words, new skills, new emotions and a myriad of other things. Everyone learns according to his or her own pace. However, not everyone has been taught a method of learning which allows his potential to be realised. The right learning method brings out the very best in us, in much the same way that an excellent teacher brings out the very best in his students.

I believe that there is a method of learning that will bring out the very best in a person and enable the person to realise his potential. I also believe that teachers in a formal and informal sense can provide us with knowledge, experience and skills. But more than this, I believe the very best teacher lies within each of us. We are, in short, our own best teachers.

A teacher or a parent may start us off on a certain path of learning, but it is ourselves who can bring out our own potential. Because I believe this with no reservations, I

xii

searched for a long time for a learning method which would give me the greatest possibility of exploring what is within me, allow me glimpses of the vast frontier which is limitless and push me forward to greater heights of achievement. To my utmost joy I have found this method of learning, and in this book I share it with you. This method of learning is called accelerative learning.

Known originally as Suggestopedia, accelerative learning and teaching was begun by a Bulgarian doctor and psychotherapist, Dr Georgie Lozanov. It was more a method of teaching rather than self learning. Suggestopedia was used initially for teaching a foreign language. It was astoundingly successful. When taught with Suggestopedia methods, Lozanov's students' learning rate was five times greater. According to Donald Schuster and Charles Gritton, well known lecturers in accelerative teaching in America, language learning has been speeded up by a factor of 3 to 1 in research undertaken there (1985). At the 1987 Suggestopedia conference held in Adelaide, Dr Sigrid Gassner-Roberts, the professor of German at Adelaide University and the leading exponent of accelerative teaching in Australia, said that Suggestopedia is seen to be the best method for teaching language by Unesco (United Nations Educational, Scientific and Cultural Organisation).

Dr Lozanov's works on this method of teaching and learning came to the west in the late sixties. In this book I have used his seminal ideas and adapted them into a programme for self accelerative learning, an aspect of Lozanov's work which has been largely neglected. In addition, I have included a chapter on how to use his teaching methods.

By applying the principles of accelerative learning, you will find that you can learn anything — from learning a foreign language to unlearning a bad habit such as smoking, from learning to rid your body of unhealthy emotions to unlearning certain psychological addictions such as a negative pattern of thinking. Last but not least, you can also learn how to be a teacher in the broadest sense of the word, that is, someone who communicates something new to another person.

In experiencing the process of accelerative learning, you will be liberated from the shackles of negative suggestions which have been implanted in us throughout our early lives. These negative suggestions remain with us for a large part of our lives unless we do something about them. It is my fervent hope that if nothing else, this book will achieve for you just that — ridding your mind of all the negative ideas about yourself and your learning ability. Until that is done, the potential which is in you cannot be realised. And if that is done, you will find, like me, that the world is a new one. It is as if you have been given a pair of new glasses and through them, what is impossible becomes possible, what is dark becomes bright, and what is a slow painful process of learning becomes joyous and accelerated.

In chapter 1 of this book, I share with you the research which has been done on the mind's potential. This is an exciting field and much is still being done by people such as Dr Barbara Brown, famed for her research on biofeedback. In chapter 2, I explain the theoretical principles underlying Dr Lozanov's ideas. Chapters 3 and 4 describe the techniques of applying these principles. Chapter 5 sets out various programmes for self accelerative learning. Chapter 6 shows you how to teach using the principles of accelerative learning. The concluding chapter points out other possible areas of learning.

How to use this book

Basically this book is about the joy intrinsic in learning. It also enables you to accelerate your learning and develop a better memory. However, none of this will occur if you do not use the book systematically. The approach taken in this book is holistic, that is, your mind and body must work together as a whole in order for you to learn in an accelerative fashion.

Globalize by reading the whole book through once. Then depending on what you have chosen to learn, go back again particularly to chapters 3, 4 and 5. Design a programme for yourself by selecting the various elements you require. After that, it is a matter of putting it into practice.

1 Your Mind's Potential and Power

The human being is a miracle. This is because of an entity known as the mind, an entity that philosophers and scientists have been trying to come to grips with, but have been relatively unsuccessful in comparison to other human ventures in the last few decades.

What the mind is we do not really know, but generally scientists equate it with the brain. A false equation, said others, notably Dr Barbara Brown, pioneer of biofeedback. She argues that the brain is not the same as the mind. The mind is not a piece of the anatomy, but the brain is. In fact, the mind directs and guides the brain just as it does other bodily functions.

That our mind can control our physiological functioning is generally accepted in today's scientific circles, but little is known about the functioning of the mind as distinct from the brain. However, what we do know of the mind now leads many scientists to claim that human potential is limitless. More specifically, it is said that the average human being uses only ten per cent of his mind. From these two statements emerge an exciting implication — the human potential awaits to be released.

If you are using only ten per cent of your mind power, then think what the possibilities are in releasing just another 50 per cent of your potential. If you are already successful and effective by using only ten per cent of your mind power, what heights could you rise to if you could release the total reserved power within you? Miracles lie ahead of you.

What is the mind then?

Dr Barbara Brown said:

> I believe I can make a solid case for the existence and potential of a superior intelligence within every Man, a

Mind-Body Power

> mind born of brain but existing apart from brain, a
> mind with extraordinary unacknowledged potency and
> range of powers. (1983:8)

This superior intelligence in each and every one of us is an
entity seen by Barbara Brown as 'the complex of innate
capacities of mind-brain to appreciate, organise, understand,
and control both body and brain' (1983, Preface).

The mind consists of the conscious and the unconscious
which together have extraordinary powers. For a long time
we have known that behind the conscious mind lies the
unconscious. The unconscious consists of a vast reservoir of
information and capacities. The unconscious acts like a giant
sponge which absorbs everything from the most trivial to the
most significant, and nothing escapes. Unlike the conscious,
the unconscious does not argue back, it does not discriminate
and, above all, it never forgets. A simple mundane experience
can testify to the efficiency of our unconscious. Many of us
have experienced times when we consciously try to remember
a name and cannot. But when engaged in other activities
totally unconnected to what we have tried to recall, the name
springs to mind.

The unconscious mind is the real power of the human
mind. Barbara Brown said, 'It was obvious then as it is today,
that the unconscious mind is the secret place of the power of
the human mind.' (1983:25) For William James, philosopher
and social psychologist, the single most important discovery
of the 20th century was Freud's discovery of the unconscious,
and the power it wields in our behaviour and personality. It is
in the unconscious that the energy resides which is capable of
producing what are seemingly impossible human feats of
endeavour. These are performed when the unconscious mind
is activated.

One of the more commonly known ways to activate the
unconscious is meditation. Take for instance the yogi who
sits on top of the Himalayan mountains right through the
winter, and emerges with a serene smile, unharmed in any
way.

Dr Herbert Benson, famed for coining the term, the

2

Your Mind's Potential Power

relaxation response, in a recent book *Beyond the Relaxation Response,* observed Tibetan monks who practise yoga. He reported that these monks, observed under western scientific control conditions, were able to change their body's temperature through meditation. In Dr Benson's own words:

> This adventure in the Himalayas has thus helped us, on one level, to define in more precise terms the power of the mind over the body. Also, the experience serves as a successful test of measuring claims of supernatural powers. Although we apparently didn't find any supernatural power, we were able to observe and explain in scientific terms a phenomenon that had been considered to be supernatural. (1985:60)

The *Australian Medical Journal* reports recently a Chinese doctor and his nephew who were lost in the snow, and who had to spend a night out in blistering winds and temperatures below freezing point. Both were found alive the next day with no ill effects. The reason — the doctor meditated throughout the night on the fire of the dragon and suffused his body with warmth which staved off certain death.

Shirley Maclaine in her book *You Can Get There From Here* recounted her experience of meditation in an extremely cold hut up in the mountains of South America. She was able to produce heat that caused her body to be soaked in perspiration by meditating on the idea of heat.

In the area of pain control, Dr Barbara Brown reports the removal of her tonsils without anaesthetics in an American operating theatre with western medical-surgical procedures. Similar observations have been made of patients operated by Chinese surgeons using acupuncture. Such operations are done without anaesthesia and the patients report no pain. These phenomena defy explanations using the concepts and theories of traditional western science. In the area of stress related symptoms and psychosomatic illnesses, even the most sceptical of medical experts will admit that these illnesses are caused by factors other than the organic. It is all in the mind of the patient. Otherwise, placebos would not be prescribed by many doctors.

Mind-Body Power

The human mind also appears to have the power to remove the causes of illness at will. Ansilie Meares, an Australian psychiatrist, practised meditation in the treatment of cancer patients and claimed many successes, as has his American counterpart, Dr Carl Simonton. Dr Simonton paid close attention to the changing of his patients' beliefs. He taught his patients to take responsibility for their own health by changing their attitudes from a victim's to a winner's. Thus the helplessness of the victim is transformed to one of personal responsibility adopted by the patients for their own recovery. Dr Simonton uses therapeutic techniques which involve mental visualisation and relaxation of body and mind. (Pritchard & Taylor, 1980)

The wide use of mental imaging or visualisation today in both western and eastern societies is testimony to the acceptance that the unconscious mind has the ability to produce results on our bodies, and change deeply entrenched habits which have defied modification on a conscious level. Dr Anthony Lazarus, author of *In the Minds: Power of Imagery for Personal Enrichment*, said: 'By using imagination it is possible to reach out to many realities that are physically absent.' (1977:5) The mind has the power to create realities which are not there. These realities in turn produce consequences in our behaviour as well as our bodies.

The Russians have harnessed the power of the mind in the development of programmes for producing excellent athletes as early as the fifties. Western observers have attributed to these programmes the Russians' ability to capture a high number of gold medals in the Olympics. In the seventies the Americans also created mind development programmes for their sportsmen and women. It is well known that Charles Tickner, the American who won the gold medal in world figure skating in 1978, used a mental programme. In the *Australian*, Australia's national newspaper, it was reported that Pat Cash, winner of the 1987 Wimbledon men's singles, used a mental programme. Ben Brass, the reporter who wrote that article, had this to say:

Because the mind and the body are inseparable, physical

4

Your Mind's Potential Power

performance will always be affected by thoughts and feelings. Athletes who don't use their minds to improve their performance risk being overtaken by those who do.

(July 11-12, 1987)

Mind-controlling-the-body phenomena are commonly reported these days, and scientific research documents systematic observations of effects of meditation undergone by yogis and practitioners of *taiji* and *qigong*. No longer dismissed as nonsense, their experiences bear testimony to the existence of a human potential which is yet to be tapped.

The supermind, a combination of your conscious and unconscious mind, is what you have. How then do we tap this potential and enable you to learn better and remember more effectively? Is there a way to develop accelerated learning and hypermnesia, that is, super memory? Is there a method that can be learned in order for you to release the stored super energy you have which will enable you to achieve the seemingly impossible?

The answer is an unqualified yes.

The objective of this book is to teach you an integrated system of learning that can unleash this potential mind power innate in you. Through this method, you learn more effectively at an accelerated rate and you can develop your mind power so that you retain information longer and better. In short, you improve your recall ability. For you, accelerative learning and super memory can be a reality.

This book tells you how.

5

2 What is Accelerative Learning?

According to Dr Lozanov, in all human beings there exist vast reserves which have not been tapped by conventional methods of learning and teaching. He defines reserves as follows:

> ...all those possibilities, known or still unknown, which are not a customary phenomenon for the average individual under given time and places.

In the definition, all of our human potential is included. Lozanov did not attempt to define the types and extent of all this human potential specifically. In his theory he only mentioned hypermnesia (super memory) and the involuntary control of the body such as psychogenic anaesthesia. However, what we do know is that Lozanov believes that all human beings have a vast repertoire of stored capacities, talents and knowledge, and this is the 90 per cent potential waiting to be released in all of us.

These potential capacities and talents can be released chiefly through unconscious mental activity. To set unconscious mental activity into motion, suggestions, both direct and indirect, play a crucial part in accelerative learning.

Accelerative learning is an integrated system of learning which combines a variety of techniques based on three main theoretical principles.

- The conscious and unconscious minds are a unity. In whatever we do, they work together as a team because the human being is an integrated whole.

- Suggestion is the means to tap the stored reserves of the human being. It is the key to unlock the potential of the mind which resides in the unconscious. It is therefore the

What is Accelerative Learning?

crucial link to accelerative learning and to super memory as well as other hyper ability.

- People learn best when they do it under conditions of pleasure, joy and relaxation. It is under such conditions that the right hemisphere of the brain is activated to work with the left hemisphere of the brain.

The right hemisphere of the brain functions in a holistic manner, processing incoming information by forming an overall pattern for them while the left is responsible for linear sequential learning. Learning and remembering is more effective when both hemispheres are used.

UNITY OF THE CONSCIOUS AND THE UNCONSCIOUS

The importance of the unconscious in the determination of our daily lives can no longer be ignored. From the smallest, most insignificant to the most momentous decisions and actions in our lives, the unconscious asserts an influence. It is as difficult to point to the unconscious as a physical entity as it is the mind. However, through inferences, we can see the workings of the unconscious.

A simple experiment engaged in by a group of psychology students as a joke on their psychology professor illustrates the power of the unconscious. Every time the professor moved to a certain corner of the room, the students looked wide awake and attentive. Every time the professor moved away from that corner, they changed their behaviour. They fidgeted, they yawned and their faces showed boredom. Before the hour was up the professor had stayed put in the corner to which the students had driven him by subtle changes in their behaviour. The professor's unconscious mind had responded to the cues provided by the students. (Barbara Brown, 1983:61)

It is remarkable how the unconscious can perform complex feats of perception and decision making, and take lines of action. Furthermore, it is able to understand meanings of social events and situations. The unconscious plays a crucial

Mind-Body Power

part in accelerative learning when combined with the use of suggestion and relaxation.

SUGGESTION

The history of suggestion goes back a long way and spans many cultures. We know for instance that some Australian aborigines practise bone pointing. When a person points a bone at someone, subsequent illness will befall that person, and often death can result.

Many doctors know that the patient's attitude towards his own illness and his will to live can determine the outcome of his illness.

In social sciences such as sociology and social psychology, we know that the person's self esteem, his identity and self concept arise from a process of socialisation which relies largely on suggestions made to the child. So if we are constantly told that we are stupid, the chances of us growing up and having a self concept centred round the key image of being a stupid person are great. And if this message is further reinforced by teachers, then the chances of us holding that particular self image are high. The self fulfilling prophecy is well known. The fact that suggestions have a powerful impact on us — our mind and body — cannot be denied.

Suggestion theory is well accepted today in hard sciences such as medicine. No longer dismissed as mysticism, suggestion theory forms the basis of hypnosis, a respectable treatment tool in some schools of psychiatry. We are capable of being hypnotised by another person such as a psychiatrist who is trained in the technique. By the same token, all human beings have an ability to make suggestions to themselves. This is known as autosuggestion.

The power of suggestion can only be inferred. We know that it has taken place only after the outcome. It is like electricity. We infer the power of electricity only after its outcome. We cannot see it.

In prescientific societies, there is strong evidence that

What is Accelerative Learning?

suggestibility factors have always been used. In the Ayurvedic and Chinese systems of medicine and philosophy, the mind over matter phenomenon is closely related to the power of suggestion. Chinese martial arts is the training of mind and body to establish man's mastery of his environment. It is a holistic system.

Accelerative learning is also a holistic approach to learning. It combines the whole body, including the brain and the mind, an entity which is a unity of the conscious and the unconscious.

In general, the term 'suggestion' has two meanings. The commonly held meaning is that suggestion is connected to hypnosis or hypnotic communication. The influence of an idea or ideas is transmitted from one person (say, the psychiatrist) to another (the patient). The recipient, in this case, the patient, accepts the idea and its influence uncritically. Furthermore, he does so mechanically. The recipient is passive, and his reasoning power is suspended while the idea is implanted in his mind. In this definition of suggestion, the recipient does things against his will. This is not the meaning of suggestion as used in accelerative learning.

Suggestion has another meaning which is used in accelerative learning. Suggestion is also indirection, hinting and intimating. It is giving an idea without explicit statements. For example, if I want my child to wash his hands before every meal, I have two options. I can tell him verbally or I can use indirection by performing the act of washing my hands every time before I sit down for a meal. When he follows my example, I can smile or reward him in other ways without making reference to my wish that he washes his hands before every meal. This type of suggestion is widely used. Good novelists use it extensively. They do not tell the readers that a person is good or bad, they convey this idea through the character's words and actions. Similarly, good playwrights do the same. They elicit the audience's response by the things shown and messages conveyed rather than the narration of the story.

Like hypnosis, accelerative learning uses suggestions to bring about certain outcomes but unlike hypnosis, it does not

Mind-Body Power

force a person to do anything against his will either because he cannot or will not use his conscious mind. This kind of suggestion gets a person to do something that he will ordinarily do anyway. In this sense, suggestion in accelerative learning is more like suggestion used in advertising. You buy something after seeing an advertisement, but you were going to do so anyway. Donald Schuster and Charles Gritton, American advocates of accelerative learning, point out the difference between the two types of suggestions used in advertising and in hypnosis in the following way:

> The difference is that suggestion in advertising attempts to persuade you to do something you might ordinarily do anyhow. Suggestion in hypnosis attempts to compel you to do some thing you ordinarily couldn't do.
>
> (1985, Preface)

The important thing to note is that when we define suggestion in the way that Schuster has, it is obvious that suggestion is present in all communication, whether we are communicating with others or with ourselves, that is, self talking. If that is the case we may as well use it to release our potential, much of which is still untapped.

RELAXATION

The process of desuggestion-suggestion works best when you are relaxed. Suggestive messages either given by yourself or by a teacher enter your unconscious more quickly and produce maximum results when you are physically and mentally relaxed. In such a state, you are free from stress, you learn with joy, interest and enthusiasm. Your motivation to learn increases.

Total relaxation comes about by the use of all our senses, that is, our sight, hearing, smell, touch and taste. The more all these senses are working together harmoniously and simultaneously, the quicker your body and mind get into a relaxed state.

10

What is Accelerative Learning?

The relaxation techniques used must therefore facilitate all the senses as well as the peripheral ones. Peripheral senses are those which we are not conscious of. For example, while looking at the writing on the blackboard, our peripheral vision can also take in the colour of the teacher's clothes, the pictures on the walls, and so on. We can also listen to the sound outside the classroom without being aware of doing so. Peripheral senses are powerful tools used by the unconscious in conjunction with the senses that we use consciously. To activate peripheral senses may require additional means of relaxation. One such means is rhythm.

Rhythm is an important natural relaxant. It is as natural as our own breathing, and it is no coincidence that rhythmic breathing is intrinsic in nearly all traditional systems of relaxation, for example, in yoga and in Chinese martial arts.

There are different types of relaxation used in accelerative learning. They can be divided into four categories, namely, physical exercises, breathing exercises, mental exercises and music. All four are integrated to produce total relaxation in a holistic way in accelerative learning. That is to say, all these exercises combine our mental and physical energy in a total way. All are especially designed and integrated to work hand in hand with suggestions with the aim of activating the unconscious in the learning process. When packaged properly, such a learning procedure results in hypermnesia (super memory) and rapid learning.

When you are relaxed in body and mind, you are more receptive so suggestions have a tendency to reach your unconscious much more efficiently. This theoretical principle is as old as yoga and *taiji* and *qigong*. Accelerative learning shares with these old systems of beliefs that as your body relaxes, your mind does too and together as a whole, you will learn better. It is through first relaxing your body (including your brain) that you get to your mind and from there tap into your unconscious.

Relaxation enables you to let go. You experience yourself as a free floating being which absorbs freely in a passive way. By letting go, it will all come. This is much like remembering a name when you have forgotten to remember it.

Mind-Body Power

THE COMMUNICATION MODEL IN ACCELERATIVE LEARNING

Now that you have understood the three theoretical principles in accelerative learning, namely, the unity of the
conscious and unconscious, suggestion and relaxation, it is
possible to describe and explain the communications model
used in this system of learning. This will enable you to see the
whole picture of your own learning process for it is only with
understanding that the desire and the ability to put theory
into application or practice is possible.

Basically whether you are a teacher or a learner, you are
engaged in a process of communicating. By definition, a
communication process is an interpersonal process. It involves two people. You may wonder how that is possible if
you are teaching yourself. After all it is only you who are
involved.

The easiest way to explain this is to tell you that all of us
are able to carry on a dialogue with ourselves. It is as if there
are two people in us. Witness, for example, a situation where
you are torn between two opposing decisions. Let us say, you
are unable to make up your mind as to whether you should
study on Sundays or join your friends and go to the movies.
Picture one particular Sunday morning when your books are
sitting in the study and the telephone is close by waiting to be
picked up so you can ring your friends. You manage to walk
into yor study and even manage to sit down by your table.
You open your book and at this stage, thoughts go through
your head. The following dialogue with a few variations
could be the result:

First voice: I should be studying, the exam. is only a
                  few weeks away.

Second voice: I still have time and I really feel like going
                  to a movie with Johnny and Marie.

First voice: But I have got so much work. I would
                  never get through all that physics. It's so
                  hard.

Second voice: The movie might relax me and it's Sunday

What is Accelerative Learning?

anyway. Who in their right mind would study on a Sunday?

First voice: Me, because I am so darned scared of failing physics. If Mr Chin is any good, I wouldn't have to study so hard at home.

Second voice: Go on, you still have so many Sundays left before the exams. You can ask Johnny and Marie to help. They are brilliant at physics. After the movie you can go home with them and do some work.

Slamming the book shut, you get up and reach for the telephone to ring your friends. Your second voice has convinced the doubting first voice. Two voices? Two people in one? There are many voices, many selves in each of us. So it is not difficult to see a teacher and student in one person. We are all a combination of learner and teacher. Insofar as you are capable of the above dialogue, and we all are, it is patently obvious that just as we can communicate with others in a myriad of verbal and nonverbal ways, we too can do the same with ourselves. Furthermore, when we communicate with others, we do so consciously and unconsciously at the same time.

When two people are engaged in communication, messages go from one to the other in a four-way system. A's conscious mind interacting with B's conscious mind is one way. The second way is A's conscious mind interacting with B's unconscious. The third way is A's unconscious interacting with B's conscious and the fourth way is A's unconscious interacting with B's unconscious. In figure 1, you will see how this process works.

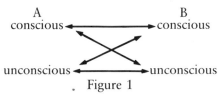

Figure 1

When a person is interacting with himself as in the case of teaching himself something, there are two levels at which he

Mind-Body Power

operates, namely, his conscious level and his unconscious level.

Within this communication model, suggestion is a constant factor. That means for every communication or interaction situation, the suggestion factor is always there. Whenever two or more people are communicating, suggestions are picked up at the conscious and unconscious levels by the people involved in the interaction. This also applies when you are interacting with yourself or what I call self interacting instead of interacting with other(s).

DESUGGESTON-SUGGESTION PROCESS

Now that you have understood the theoretical principles involved in accelerative learning, we can examine the process of suggestion and desuggestion. In order to learn in an accelerative fashion, it is important for you to empty your mind and self of all the blocks against learning which you have acquired throughout your life. These are barriers to learning. Until you get rid of these barriers, you will not be able to let in the positive suggestions and make them activate your unconscious. In other words, until you get rid of your resistance to learning, your potential cannot be unleashed.

It is necessary for you to empty out the old to make room for the new to enter. The old consists of all the beliefs and experiences you have acquired so far in your life. These may be beliefs that learning is always difficult and it has always been a struggle with little result. It may be that you once had a rotten teacher who punished you every time you made a mistake. To this day, I hate sewing in a classroom situation because I had a terrible teacher who used to send me out of class for every sewing lesson. If your experiences have been like mine, you will have to desuggest these negative experiences out of your mind and start anew.

Yet another very powerful block is to do with your self concept. If you have been constantly told that you are stupid, you may have already internalised a view of yourself as such. You may have little confidence in your own learning ability

14

What is Accelerative Learning?

and other capabilities. How many times have you said: 'I can't do that. It's too difficult.'?

Barriers to Learning

In accelerative learning there are three types of barriers to learning that have been identified by Lozanov. They are:

- the logical barrier
- the intuitive-emotional barrier
- the moral-ethical barrier

If a suggestion is made which is illogical, then you will reject it. For example, if you are placed last in the class and you are told that you are as smart as the rest of the students, you may say to yourself: 'If I am as smart as the rest of the class, how come I am placed last?' So you reject this suggestion on logical grounds.

The intuitive-emotional barrier has to do with your confidence and emotional security. Suggestions which threaten your sense of security and confidence will be rejected by you. Alternatively, suggestions counteracting something about which you feel strongly may be rejected. So for example, if you have always hated physics, then you will resist the suggestion that it will be enjoyable and that you will like it. The uneasy feeling that we sometimes get although we cannot find any logical reasons for it is possibly one of the best indications that our intuitive-emotional barrier is operating.

The moral-ethical barrier has to do with your ethical principles. This barrier goes up when suggestions are contradictory to, or violate, your sense of right and wrong in some way. For example, you will not continue reading this book and learn from it if it violates your religion or your sense of decency in some way.

These three anti-suggestive barriers intertwine and mutually interact very closely. It is impossible to separate them from each other. These barriers can never be destroyed totally in

15

Mind-Body Power

the individual as they are protective mechanisms. Instead, incoming suggestions must harmonise with them and when they do, these suggestions can be translated into effects. As Lozanov said:

> The more a suggestion harmonises with the logical requirements of the personality, the intuitive-affective and ethical components of the personality, the quicker and the easier is the suggestion realised.   (1978)

How long it takes to overcome these barriers vary from individual to individual. It may take days. It may take months. Or it can occur immediately. Overcoming the anti-suggestive barriers cannot be brought about by force or coercion of any kind. It can only take place through a process of psychological harmonisation between the incoming suggestions and the individual.

In summary, the desuggestion-suggestion process begins by eliminating old blocks or preconceived ideas to learning. New suggestions can then operate on the unconscious. Suggestions reach your unconscious far quicker when you are in a state of relaxation. When all these have been successful, accelerative learning takes place because your untapped reserves are unlocked.

Figure 2 gives you a picture of how the desuggestion-suggestion process operates.

Barriers to Learning
↓
Desuggestions + Suggestions
New Suggestions (input under conditions of
relaxation)
↓
Activating Unconscious
↓
Untapped Potential (Accelerative Learning +
Super Memory)

Figure 2

What is Accelerative Learning?

SUMMARY AND IMPORTANT POINTS TO REMEMBER

- Learning takes place on the conscious and unconscious level.

- Suggestion is a constant factor in all communication.

- Learning only takes place when barriers are removed and new positive suggestions are fed in.

- Learning is most effective when carried out under conditions of relaxation and joy.

REVISION

1 What are the three theoretical principles of accelerative learning?

2 Describe how they are all linked together.

3 Describe the desuggestion-suggestion process.

Exercise 1 *Barriers to Learning*

List on a piece of paper all the negative things that you believe about yourself and your ability to learn. For example:

1 I have always found it really impossible to learn a language.

2 Other people can learn things so quickly but me, no way. I must be dumb.

3 Don't ask me to learn to sing — I am tone deaf.

After you have done that, list all the positive things. For example:

1 I am able to read this book. I have learnt how to read and write. Can't be that dumb after all.

2 I can whistle.

17

Mind-Body Power

3 I have learnt to dress nicely.

Now look over the two lists and compare them. Are they balanced? Are there more negatives over positives? If so, go back and continue with the positive list until it has more statements than your negative list.

Make three positive statements about learning in general, eg, *anyone can learn any thing; I can learn something new — I have done it before* (your positive list confirms this).

⧉ Relaxation

Relaxation is a vital condition for the desuggestion-suggestion process to work. In order to accelerate your learning progress, your mind and body, in fact, your total being, must be relaxed, for it is in the state of relaxation that you feel secure and joyous. Total relaxation in mind and body brings these rewards involuntarily.

There is some physiological basis for this. According to Dr James Hand, Assistant Dean at the Illinois College of Medicine, who has carried out research on the brain and its role in accelerative learning, the brain produces chemicals which can generate positive, good feeling when we enjoy something and negative feeling when we wish to avoid something (1986). The chemicals referred to by Dr Hand are endorphin and encephalin. Both produce good feelings. It is known now that relaxation enables the brain to release these chemicals.

When relaxed there is no doubt that you find that you tend to remember things better than when you are tense and anxious. For instance, how many times have you 'forgotten' simply because you were tensed up trying to remember? How many times have you read a page over again and again and not take in a single word because you are worried about something?

From the research done on stress management we know that when a person is stressed, a number of consequences follow: the person tends to distort realities, what have been perceived as possibilities become impossibilities, what have been strengths become weaknesses, in short, the person loses confidence. And confidence is the vital ingredient in accelerative learning. If you believe you can do it, you can. This positive mental state, this optimism, is only present when your stress level is low.

Mind-Body Power

To bring about total relaxation, four types of relaxation techniques are used in accelerative learning. These are: music, physical exercise, breathing exercise and mental exercise.

MUSIC

Music is nourishment for our conscious and unconscious. Music, as shown in more recent research, seems to be fed to our body apart from our mind. Dr Steve Halpern, composer, performer and pioneer in the field of sound health — ie, the study of noise and its negative impact on our health, and the use of sound in health therapies — has this to say:

> We hear and ingest sounds with more than our auditory mechanism. The whole body responds to sound and consumes it whether we consciously hear the sound or not. Consider how the mind tunes out the ticking of a clock or the humming of a refrigerator. But even though the conscious mind can filter out the sound, the body cannot. (1985:38)

Music has always been with us. It existed before mankind. Pause for a moment and listen to the singing of birds, the rustling of leaves, the sighs of the wind, the crescendoes of the waves. Pause. Listen to the sound of the silences on top of the mountains and in depths of oceans. Yes, music has always been here. Within our bodies, there is also music. There is rhythm and beat. The vital organ, our heart, on an average beats to a tempo of 70 to 80 beats per minute. Rhythm is innate in us. A newborn child without being taught can follow the rhythm of music. The songs that rise from our throats come from deep wells of our being.

Steve Halpern believes that our bodies 'create and resonate to vibrations'. He claims that the entire body as a total system vibrates at a rate of approximately 7.8 to 8 cycles per second when it is at its most naturally relaxed state. The frequency of the brain waves is also 8 cycles per second when a person is in a state of meditation. This is no accident according to

Relaxation

Halpern because as he says, 'physicists have shown that the earth itself vibrates at this same fundamental frequency of 8 cycles per second ... The nervous systems of all life forms are attuned to this fundamental frequency. Thus there is a resonance between the human instrument in a natural relaxed state and the electrically charged layers of the earth's atmosphere ... the phrase "being in harmony with oneself and the universe" might be more than a beautiful, poetic image.' (1985:39)

The implications of Steve Halpern's research writings are profound for accelerative learning. They certainly lend strong support to what Lozanov has claimed — that music must be an intrinsic part of learning, for it brings about a state of relaxation in the person which in turn activates the unconscious.

Lozanov has done years of research on the type of music which is suitable for accelerative learning. This is basically Baroque music with a largo tempo, that is 60 beats to a minute with a measure of 4/4. The relaxation comes about because of the synchronisation of our body rhythms. The tempo of 60 beats gradually slows down our heart rate and the measure of 4/4 slows down our breathing to approximately 15 breaths per minute. It looks like our body moves involuntarily to music we listen to.

Baroque music is essentially a European music and if you are not used to it, you might find it strange at first. If you do, the only substitution for it is Steve Halpern's music which I have used and found to have the same effect. In fact, Steve Halpern's music has an oriental flavour, not unlike Chinese music played with classical instruments such as the pipa, although Steve Halpern uses modern electronic equipment.

Research is still going on in the area of music and accelerative learning. Although I believe that music is a matter of taste and often it is relative to the culture from which it has emerged, in our current state of knowledge regarding music used in accelerative learning, I am reluctant to say experiment with other music. Not all music is relaxing although it can be entertaining. A lot of people say they listen to music to relax. Research has shown that rock music and

Mind-Body Power

disco music, for instance, produce a negative impact on the person.

> The rhythm of much rock music may tend to override the more subtle signals of the body's own communication system. The end result is that the body's system is confused, the heart's response is irregular, and the body gets weakened.
>
> (Halpern, 1985:70)

There is another reason for using Baroque music and not other forms of popular music when you are learning. In accelerative learning, music serves to relax and helps you move towards the unconscious part of your mind more easily. However, music with which you can hum along or sing along easily can distract your attention. So for the purpose of accelerating learning or improving your retentive ability, it is also best not to be over familiar with the particular piece of music. As soon as you are, change it and use something else.

Make Your Own Music

As the tempo of 60 minutes is the crucial element in this type of music, it is possible to make your own music if you have a metronome. Find a deserted beach, then set your metronome needle on largo and a measure of 4/4 or 2/4. Tape the beat of the metronome against the backdrop sound of the waves. This is very effective mood creating music. Likewise, a metronome by a waterfall can be equally effective.

If it is difficult for you to find a deserted beach, running a shower is a good substitute in simulating the sound of a waterfall. If you do not live by the beach or waterfall, hills, mountains and forests can also provide natural music — birds singing, wind rustling in the leaves. Again leave a metronome in a quiet spot and tape it.

Relaxation

Mood Creating Music

I have advised that you should not use all kinds of music to relax and learn by. However, if you want to memorise some materials when learning a particular topic which is obviously related to a certain type of culture, it can be very effective if you use some music to create the atmosphere that is suggestive of that particular culture. It is especially so in the learning of languages. When you are learning Chinese, for example, it would be useful to play a Chinese melody as a preliminary mood creating device. Chinese folk songs can also be used. However, in the actual process of learning Chinese vocabulary, you must switch back to Baroque music.

In accelerative learning, music is used for two other purposes apart from creating the right mood for the materials to be learnt. One purpose is for the active concert phase when your brain waves are operating at beta level, that is, when you are alert and wide awake. The active concert is a phase when you can play a more dramatic type of music. Any lively classical music which tends to excite and stimulate your imagination in developing images and 'messages' is suitable for the active concert phase.

The other purpose is to use music for the pseudo passive concert. Here you are relaxed but focused and your brain waves are operating on alpha level. The pseudo passive concert requires the use of Baroque largo music. You sit passively, apparently doing nothing behaviourially yet you take in what is being seen and heard. You are behaviourally passively, apparently doing nothing behaviourally; yet, you take in what is being seen and heard. You are behaviourally materials emotionally and intuitively. So for example, at this phase if you are trying to read and memorise the important points of a business report, you will put on a piece of Baroque largo music (eg Vivaldi's *Winter from Four Seasons*) and read passively without active and conscious exertion, much like the attitude adopted when you are at a concert. In short, it is an attitude of sitting back and relaxing yet paying attention. It is in this sense that this phase is known as the pseudo passive concert. The pseudo passive concert is a vital

Mind-Body Power

component in the process of committing materials to memory.

See the appendix for lists of music pieces which can be used during your accelerative learning sessions.

BREATHING EXERCISES

Breathing is part of the natural rhythm of your body. It is also life. When your breathing is not right, your body does not feel right. Thus it is important that you learn to breathe in such a way that you can relax your body and mind. With practice, it is surprising how easy this is.

Find a place that is quiet and away from interruptions (eg tv or telephone). Soft, slow music, preferably Baroque in largo, often helps in relaxing most people very quickly. Closing your eyes helps you to focus inward and rest your mind.

Remember not to force your breathing, that is, when inhaling, do not take one big gulp of air, and when exhaling, do not let out one big sigh. Breathe naturally. Learn to be aware of your breathing and the movements in your body as you breathe.

Deep Breathing

Posture sit on a chair with your back straight and place both feet flat on the floor. Place your hands loosely on your abdomen and close your eyes. Check that you are not clenching your teeth, jaws or face.

- Slowly take in a deep breath. Let it go down to your abdomen. Your abdomen should fill up like a balloon.
- Pause.
- Slowly exhale. Your abdomen should deflate.

Rhythmic Breathing

Rhythmic breathing requires you to breathe with a certain rhythm. Usually this is done in cycles of various counts. To

Relaxation

begin with, you should do the breathing in counts of 2, increase it to 4 and then 6. As you get better with it, you can slow down your breathing even more.

Posture   sit comfortably with your back straight.
- Close your eyes.
- Breathe in counting mentally, 1, 2.
- Pause 1, 2.
- Breathe out counting 1, 2.
- Pause 1, 2.

This constitutes 1 cycle of breathing. Do 10 cycles.

Focused Breathing

Posture   sit comfortably with your back straight. Alternatively lie down flat on your back with a pillow.
- Close your eyes.
- Breathe normally and as you do so, gaze with your mind's eye at each part of your body. As you gaze on each part, breathe into it to a count of 4. Begin with your forehead, proceed to your eyes, ears, nose, chin, neck and down to the rest of your body.

PHYSICAL EXERCISES

Physical exercise relaxes the body and brings about good physiological results. For accelerative learning, the inclusion of physical exercise keeps the body and mind relaxed and alert. Try to do the exercises below without straining yourself. For those who have not done physical exercise for a long time, the first few times may be strenuous and you may experience some slight pain and aches. However, that is normal to begin with. Regular practice every day will get rid of these aches.

The exercises described below are easy and gentle. You should be able to do them with no problems regardless of your age. They are deliberately named to suggest a picture in your mind as you do them. In this way, they are easier for you to remember. The number of times you choose to repeat them

25

Mind-Body Power

for each learning session is up to you. It all depends on how much time you have. A general guideline is that you should do these physical exercises as a start to your learning session for approximately ten minutes.

Loving Yourself

Posture Stand comfortably with your arms loosely hanging on your sides. Keep your back straight but relaxed.

- *Eyes* — keeping your head still, move your eyes to the right as far as they can go then back to centre. Move your eyes to left as far as they can go, then back to centre. Repeat both movements 10 times.
- *Neck* — breathing in, turn your neck slowly to the right. Breathing out, return your neck to the centre. Breathing in, turn your neck slowly to the left. Breathing out, return your neck to the centre. Repeat these 2 movements 10 times.
- *Arms* — breathing in, raise both arms above your head and stretch. Breathing out, drop both

arms and loosen entire body. Do these 2 movements 10 times.

- *Shoulders* — breathing normally, rotate both shoulders in a clockwise direction. Do this 10 times.
- *Waist* — put your hands on your waist. Breathing in twist the upper part of your body to the right. Hold for 4 seconds. Breathing out, return to the centre. Breathing in, turn to the left, hold for 4 seconds. Breathing out return to centre position. Do this 10 times.
- *Thighs* — keeping your back straight, breathing in, lower yourself down to an imaginary chair. Holding your breath sit on this imaginary chair for 4 seconds. Breathing out, stand up slowly. Repeat 10 times.

26

Relaxation

- *Knees* — bend forward slightly and place your hands on your knees. Feel the knobs of your knees in your palms. Press these knobs and rub them in a rotating motion to a count of 10. Straighten back to normal standing posture. Open your eyes.
- *Ankles* — breathing normally, lift your right foot slightly from the floor. Rotate your foot first clockwise 10 times, then anti-clockwise 10 times. Repeat this for the left foot.
- Close your eyes. Breath normally. Take your gaze inward. Mentally travel down from your head to your toe. Then travel from your toe back to your head. This is a mental check to see that every muscle is relaxed.
- *Stretch* — breathing in deeply, and still keeping your eyes closed, lift both arms above your head and stretch. Imagine that you are a cat stretching. Then cross your arms and wrap them around yourself, giving yourself a big hug. Clasp tightly. Tighten clasp. Rock gently from side to side and say 'I love myself.' Say this 10 times. Open your eyes and feel marvellous.

Monkey Swings From Tree to Tree

Visualise a monkey swinging from tree to tree. *Posture* stand with your feet slightly apart. Hang arms loosely on your sides. Breathe normally.
- Twisting your waist to the left, swing both arms to the left. Repeat for the right side.

Mind-Body Power

Flower Opening to Greet the Sun

Visualise a flower opening and closing its petals as you do this exercise.

Posture stand with your feet slightly apart.

- Cross your arms, put your right hand on left shoulder and left hand on your right shoulder as if you are hugging yourself.
- Drop your head.
- Inhale, stretch your arms slowly towards the sun and lift your head at the same time.
- Exhale, bring your arms back to their original position.

Bamboo Bending in the Breeze

Visualise a supple bamboo bending left and right in the breeze.

Posture stand with feet slightly apart.

- Inhale, raise your right arm above the head keeping it in a straight line with your body.
- Exhale, bend sideways to the left from your waist, keeping knees straight.

- Straighten up, lower right arm and relax.
- Repeat with left arm.

Relaxation

Kingfisher Beside the Sea

Visualise a kingfisher standing very still beside the water's edge.
Posture stand upright, feet together.
- Raise your right foot and hold your toes with your right hand. Your toes would be bent backwards.
- Raise your left hand straight above your head. Inhale and stretch.
- Relax and return to original position.
- Repeat with right hand holding left foot.

Kangaroo Touching Its Toes

Visualise a kangaroo standing in the middle of a vast clearing in the evening sun.
Posture stand with feet slightly apart, arms hanging loose by the sides.
- Inhale, lift both arms above head.
- Bend, touch your left toes with your right hand.
- Exhale, return to original posture.
- Repeat movement to touch your right toes with your left hand.

Seagull Stretches Its Wings

Visualise a seagull standing on the seashore, its feathers white and glistening in the sun.

Posture stand with feet apart.

- Inhaling, raise and stretch arms sideways to the height of your shoulder. Raise right foot to the height of your left knee. Hold to a count of 4 seconds.
- Exhaling, lower foot back to original position.
- Do the same for left foot.

Bat Hangs From a Branch

Visualise a bat hanging from a tree branch.

Posture stand straight with feet together.

- Lift both arms above your head and lace your fingers, palms downwards.
- Rise on your toes and as you do this, turn your laced fingers to face the sky.
- Lower your toes and turn your fingers downwards.
- Drop arms to your sides and relax.

Relaxation

Kitten Plays Tug-of-war

Visualise a playful kitten struggling with a ball of red wool.

Posture stand with your feet slightly apart.

- Raise your hands to waist level with palms facing away from your body as if you are pushing against something.
- Turn your body slightly to the left. Push forward wih your body, bending your left knee slightly.
- Repeat for right side.

Grasshopper Hula Hoops

Visualise a green grasshopper standing in the middle of a field.

Posture stand with your feet apart and knees slightly bent.

- Put your hands on your waist. Rotate you hips clockwise to a count of 10.
- Repeat in an anti-clockwise direction.

Willow Weeps Over River

Visualise the graceful willow tree, its leaves and branches bending over a river.

Posture   stand with your feet slightly apart.
- Swing your arms behind and put hands together.
- Inhale, bend forward with knees straight.
- Exhale, return to upright position.

Water Carrier Lifting Buckets

Visualise a person with a long pole sitting on his shoulders. With this pole he picks up two buckets of water, one at each end.

Posture   stand with feet apart.
- Raise your arms sideways to shoulder level with palms opening facing the floor.
- Bend sideways to the right as if the bucket of water on that side is heavier.
- Return to upright position.
- Repeat for left side.

Relaxation

Turtle On Its Back

Visualise a turtle on its back trying to turn over.
Posture lie with your back flat on the floor and your arms relaxed by your sides, palms open, touching floor.
- Inhale, draw both knees up, keeping your feet firmly planted on the floor.
- Pressing your feet and palms against the floor, inhale and push your abdomen upwards.
- Exhale and return to original position.
- Repeat 10 times.

Crocodile Flicks Its Tail

Visualise a crocodile lying in the warmth of a tropical sun.
Posture lie flat on your stomach. Rest your chin on your hands, arms raised from the elbow.
- Inhale, lift your right leg.
- Exhale, lower it.
- Repeat for left leg.
- Repeat, lifting both legs each time.

Fish Sunning Its Belly

Visualise a slippery shiny fish swimming in clear blue waters on its back.
Posture   lie flat on your back. Put your hands under your buttocks with your palms pressed against the floor.

- Inhale, raise your chest slowly, pushing your hands against the floor. Stay in this position to a count of 4 seconds.

- Exhale and return to original position.

Cobra Raises Its Head

Visualise a cobra suddenly hearing a disturbing noise.
Posture   lie flat on your stomach. Place your palms on the floor near your shoulders.

- Inhale, push your hands against the floor and raise your head and shoulders together while the lower part of your body remains in contact with the floor. Stay in this position to a count of 4 seconds.

- Exhale and return to original position.

Relaxation

Tiger Yawns In the Morning

Imagine a tiger that has just woken up.
Posture crouch on fours, hands pressed on the floor with arms straight.
- Inhale, arch your back.
- Exhale through your mouth and straighten your back.
- Close your mouth and return to original position.

Chicken Draws Circles With Its Feet

Visualise a chicken playing in the farmyard.
Posture sit on the floor with your back straight and with legs stretched out in front. Place your hands by your sides, pressed against the floor.
- Lift right foot 6 inches off the floor and rotate clockwise to a count of 10.
- Repeat in an anti-clockwise direction.
- Repeat exercise with left foot.

Ostrich Shows Its Tail

Visualise an ostrich bent over eating grass.
Posture   squat with feet apart.
- Press your palms against the floor in front of you.
- Push your bottom up while keeping your palms flat on the floor. Your knees can be bent slightly. Keeping your feet still, 'walk' with your hands in front of you.
- 'Walk' your hands backwards to original position.

Caterpillar Uncurls Its Body

Visualise a fat green caterpillar contentedly stretched on a leaf.
Posture   lie with your back flat on the floor.
- Inhale, pull your knees towards your chest with legs bent. Clasp bent legs with your arms.
- Exhale, raise your head to meet your knees. Hold for 4 seconds.
- Stretch out and return to original position.

Mind-Body Power

MENTAL EXERCISE

Exercises to relax mentally are important to your mind and will help you to accelerate learning. Basically mental exercises rely on your imagination which can use all your five senses — sight, hearing, touch, taste and smell. The more efficiently these senses are used to bring up an image, the better it is for your learning process.

Mental exercises calm your mind and empty it of thoughts which act as obstacles to your learning. Your unconscious mind never rests even when you are asleep. Otherwise you cannot dream. Dreams spring from your unconscious. Always choose scenes or situations, events or people who have a relaxing effect on you. Images, places and things vary from individual to individual in terms of their power to act as mind relaxants. You know what best relaxes your mind, what scenes can be most easily conjured up to put you into a state of relaxation. Do not be afraid to use them.

The following three steps should always be used before you begin your mind calming exercises.

- Find a place and time suitable for you.

- Get into a comfortable position either sitting or lying down. Stand if you prefer that.

- Close your eyes.

The Sea

Now start imagining that you are walking towards the sea. You can feel the sand under your bare feet. As you approach the sea, its shimmering waters beckon to you. You hear the gentle lap, lap of the waves inviting you to enter. The smell of fresh air wafts up to your nostrils. You enter the water, its coolness washing over your skin. You float gently on the water, feeling very relaxed, feeling that all your tensions are dissolving in the water. It is a good feeling. Now you are completely relaxed, your body seems to dissolve into the water. The water and you are one movement. You breathe

Mind-Body Power

slowly, in, out, in, out. You are relaxed, so relaxed. So relaxed that you can learn anything, remember anything.

Watching the Trees

You enter a coconut grove in the early hours of the morning. Sunshine filters through, soft and gentle. You sink down onto the ground, keeping your eyes on the sunlight through the coconut fronds. Slowly you spread out on the soft ground and lie flat on your back. As you watch the sunlight through the fronds, your eyelids get heavy with relaxation. Your eyelids get heavier and heavier and you close your eyes. You feel the sunshine on your face. You hear silence in the grove. Peaceful, so peaceful. Relaxing. The sun grows warmer, your body feels lighter. Your tensions slip away from your body into the ground. Tensions slip away, away....

Floating On a Cloud

You are lying on your back in a field. You smell the freshness of grass. In the distance, faintly, you hear the singing of birds. Sunshine warms your face. As your stare up at the clear blue sky, a cloud drifts by. You follow this ball of white fluffiness with your eyes — follow it as it drifts further and further into the horizon. You feel soft and relaxed, drifting just like the little cloud across the sky. Your arms get heavy with relaxation, your legs grow heavy, first your right leg, then your left. Your body feels heavier and heavier. Your mind is clear and white, like a cloud, clear and white ... clear and white....

Throwing Pebbles

You are perched on a rock. You stare at the river. Your eyes watch the current flow downwards towards the sound of a rushing waterfall. You pick up a pebble and throw it into the river. It makes a soft 'plop' sound. You pick up another pebble and throw ... and another.... Your arm feels heavy, it gets heavier and heavier as you throw one pebble after

Relaxation

another. Soon your shoulders get heavy with relaxation, then your neck, then down your spine, then your right leg, your right toes, your left leg and toes. You feel relaxed all over ... all over....

4   Creative Visualisation

In the previous chapter you have learnt relaxation techniques which provide the right conditions for the desuggestion-suggestion process to work most efficiently. In conjunction with relaxation techniques creative visualisation must also be used. Relaxation techniques and creative visualisation work hand in hand to tap the unconscious so that the mental reserves of the individual can be released. In this chapter you will learn how to use creative visualisation to accelerate learning. It is easy to learn and requires little time to practise.

Creative visualisation is the means with which you make suggestions to yourself. These suggestions can reach into your unconscious when you are in a relaxed state and consists largely of the mind's eye creating mental images.

Creative visualisation must be learnt whether you are going to teach yourself or teach others. It is by doing the exercises yourself that it is possible for you to empathise with the learner, to flow with the learner's feelings and pace.

MENTAL IMAGING

Before beginning bear in mind that our consciousness is directed to our five senses — our hearing, sight, smell, taste and touch. These provide sensory stimulation and the more we make use of them in a holistic or total way, the more effective we are in our learning on a conscious level. By the same token, if we are trying to work on our unconscious, then it is equally important that all these five senses must be resorted to. When you are doing the following creative visualisation exercises, make sure you use all your five senses as much as possible.

40

Creative Visualisation

SIMPLE CREATIVE VISUALISATION

The first thing to do is simply find a quiet place for yourself. A room in which you have habitually found peace and quiet is always a good start. If you cannot find a quiet room for yourself in the house, a spot outdoors will do as well, such as a place on a beach or in a park. When I was a child in Malaya, I always found a corner in a temple near my home a very good place in which to daydream and write stories in my head. Churches, when there are no services, also make excellent places for creative visualisation. So do not despair if your house is full of relatives or an endless stream of visitors. There are always other places to go to for peace and quiet.

Having found a place which is suggestive of relaxation, sit comfortably with your back straight and relaxed. A straight back often prevents you from dropping off to sleep. Let us practise a simple visualisation exercise to begin with.

Close your eyes and breathe normally. Check to make sure that no part of your body is tensed. Check in particular your jaws — make sure that they are not clenched. Also, make sure your neck and muscles between your shoulder blades are not tensed.

When you are comfortable and feeling at ease, let your mind wander. Thoughts will come in and out. Let them. After a while, visualise yourself as you are sitting there. Examine how you feel sitting there quietly. Does it feel good? Peaceful? Switch from that image to a picture of your house. Can you see it? What colour is it? Enter your house through the front door. Walk through it to the back. Leave by the back door. Walk to your school. Visualise the journey. What can you see on the way? Focus your mind's eye on these objects — cars, buses, bicycles, people, trees, houses. Is there a particular landmark, perhaps a post office? Focus your gaze on it. See the colours of the building, its shape, is it square, rectangular?

If your house and school do not conjure up pleasant relaxing memories, switch to other objects which are more pleasant. These objects can be people or pets. Taking your dog for a walk by the river bank is a simple effective

41

Mind-Body Power

visualisation exercise if you have a dog and have walked it before.

Another visualisation exercise for beginners could be the reenacting of a story or film you have seen recently. Take the story *Cinderella* for example. Visualise the first scene — Cinderella with a broom in her hand sweeping the kitchen floor while the stepsisters and stepmother jeer and scold her. Picture the whole story scene by scene until the very end when the prince comes to put the slipper on Cinderella's foot. What colours do you see? What are the sounds? What music is playing at the ball?

If you have tried out these simple exercises for a few times, you can now start to do more complex ones which are directed towards a goal which you wish to achieve.

GOAL ACHIEVEMENT EXERCISE

Find a quiet place, sit comfortably and close your eyes. Now put in your mind a goal that you want to accomplish such as passing an examination with high distinctions. Be very clear in your mind what the goal is. Dwell on it for a while. Is it just passing the examination or is it passing the examination with high distinctions? If you are undecided, do not go on to the next step until you have made up your mind.

Next, start to visualise. See in your mind the accomplishment of the goal you have set yourself. Take yourself to that situation — the place and the time. Visualise everything in that situation as much as possible. Is it a sunny day? Yes. You can feel the sunshine on your skin, on your head. When you reach to touch your head, it feels warm. How do you feel? Happy? Joyous? Elated? Let these feelings engulf you. Sink into these wonderful feelings of achievement. How is your heart behaving? Is it thumping with excitement? And your stomach — what sensations can you experience? Butterflies having a ball? Listen to your breathing. Is is quicker, shorter? Do sounds rise from your throat? *Whoopie, I passed my exams with distinctions*, you shout. Someone hears you — who is it? Your mother, she hears you. You hear her

Creative Visualisation

laughing, see her face smiling and you feel marvellous. You have done it.

At some stage in your visualisation, doubts will creep in to try and sabotage you. These doubts take the form of statements like: *Don't be a fool. You know you can't do it.* Or *What if I fail?* Don't worry when these doubts arise to cloud your concentration in visualising your goal. Deliberately let the doubts set in. Dwell on them and deal with them one by one. This is part of the total visualisation exercise and constitutes the second stage. Doubts can be conscious and unconscious. When they rise from your unconscious they can be very powerful and have to be dealt with. So it is best to tackle them while you are doing your visualisation. That is when you are tapping your unconscious anyway.

In dealing with doubts, be very firm and take control of the doubting voice coming from inside you. Unless you master it, it will master you. Greater people than us have experienced hearing this voice so do not let it get you down. Certainly do not let that doubting voice take over your life. Argue with it. For example, 'I'll fail' can be countered with 'No, I won't. Why should I?'

When you have successfully dealt with that doubting inner voice, you are ready to proceed to the third stage of your visualisation. Revisualise your goal. State it clearly again. Then state the reason why you want the goal. For example, you want to pass your examinations with distinctions because you want to go to university. Now tell yourself what you can do once your goal is accomplished. You can say something like this: 'After going to university, I can earn my own living and be of help to mum and dad.'

The fourth stage of your visualisation deals with a rational plan on how to accomplish your goal in the real world. What do you have to do first? And next? You may have to study very hard. And how can you do this? By cutting down on watching television and going to parties every Saturday night. Figure out one step after another until you are satisfied with the overall plan to accomplish your stated goal.

Having done that, open your eyes and do not think about the accomplishment of your goal. Your unconscious will set

Mind-Body Power

to work. You will find that you will watch television less and, in fact, lose interest in it without knowing why. You will study harder without great difficulty. You will accomplish your goal.

EXERCISE TO GET RID OF WORRY

Three of the most powerful obstacles to effective learning are worry, anxiety and fear of not getting what we want. All three emotions prevent us from relaxing and therefore effectively freeze our conscious and unconscious minds, preventing accelerative learning to take place. Here is an exercise you can use whenever you are feeling worried.

Find a quiet place and sit comfortably. Close your eyes. Breathe normally. Now think about what is worrying you. Let it come clearly and strongly into your mind. For example, if it is worry about not passing an approaching examination then think about it. How do you feel now? Worried, yes, but still not too bad. You are healthy and can still think rationally. Right?

Now switch to another image. You have actually failed the examination. How do you feel? Go deep into the feelings of anguish, depression and disappointment. Even disgrace. How does your body feel? Do you have a headache? A pain in your chest maybe? Now ask yourself what could possibly be the worst thing that can happen to you now that you have failed the examination. Go through the possibilities one by one. Now visualise a telephone call from your doctor telling you that you have cancer and only a month to live. Think about failing the examination and your imminent death. Visualise which is more important.

Listen to your own heart beat deliberately. What does this tell you? This tells you that you are still alive. And in the end, that is all that matters. You will also discover that having gone through all the terrible things in your visualisation, they do not seem to matter that much in comparison with your life being threatened.

Creative Visualisation

EARLY PLEASANT LEARNING RESTIMULATION EXERCISE

This is one of the loveliest creative visualisation exercises that anyone can do. Basically it is an exercise which takes you back to a time in your past when you have enjoyed learning something. By using that pleasant moment or situation, you recreate the same feelings for whatever you are learning in the present. It is in its simplest form an association of two separate occasions of learning — the past and the present.

Go somewhere quiet. Sit comfortably and breathe normally. Close your eyes. When you are relaxed, think of a time or a situation when you have enjoyed learning something new. This could be your first attempts to swim. This could be a time in your life long ago when you learned to eat an ice cream out of a cone without it falling off. It could be a recent learning situation eg when you put on your jogging shoes and learned to exercise in a park and became a member of the fitness fraternity. As long as it was fun, you can use it.

Some people find it really difficult to think of a single thing which they have enjoyed learning. If you are one of these people, think of the first time you learnt to sit in a cinema and enjoy a film. Or the time when you read your first story book or novel. It must be something that you have enjoyed doing, not simply the achievement of it.

A good example to illustrate the difference between the joy intrinsic in the learning process itself and the joy in the end result of this process is watching children who are learning to swim on their own. There they are splashing and laughing, little arms waving widely and chubby legs kicking everywhere. The sound of their laughter and the splashing of the water intermingle. The sunshine on their fine smooth skins make them glisten like silvery fish. Have you ever watched this scene before? Well, what is happening? These children are simply enjoying the process of learning to swim on their own. The end result of this process is gaining the ability to swim. The two are linked — the first leading to the second.

Thus when you are thinking of an enjoyable learning experience in the past, make sure your enjoyment was in the process of learning itself and not simply the outcome of that

Mind-Body Power

process. My guess is that if you have enjoyed learning, then you have achieved the result of that learning process itself. The first novel which I had read from cover to cover was Wilkie Collins' *The Lady in White*. I was 11. I will never forget that experience and even now as I write this, I feel the excitement, anticipation and joy of being engaged in the reading process itself — my fingers turning the pages, my eyes devouring the words, faster and faster. The end result of that process is my ability to read a novel. There was also a bonus. My passion for reading was developed.

Now that you understand what you have to do, you can start to let yourself flow into the past learning situation that you have chosen. Recall it vividly. Recall it in a total way, with your mind and your body.

Recreate the scene. What are you doing? Where are you? What is around you? Who is with you? What can you see? What can you hear? What can you smell?

Go through the experience with your body now. How does your body feel? Is your heart pumping with excitement? Is your stomach tight? Your throat, how does it feel? Your eyes, are they widening in anticipation?

Let yourself go right into the sensations of your body. Go into your feelings deeply.

Now think of something new that you want to learn for the present, whether learning a new language, how to cook or learning to ride a bicycle, and so on. Think about it. How keen are you in learning this new thing? Do you really want to do it? If the answer is yes, then say to yourself:

> I can do it. It is fun, just like my past experience of learning ...... (fill in whatever you have chosen earlier). I feel exactly the same happiness, joy and pleasure and it is just like that. Very easy.

Say these statements with conviction. And there is no reason why you cannot. After all, if you have done it once, then you can do it again.

46

Creative Visualisation

MEMORY IMPROVEMENT EXERCISE

This is an exercise which you can use if you want to remember a list of things. The idea is to create an image for each of the things, each image fitting in with the other in the form of a story. Below are listed 20 words.

chair
house
tree
book
duck
boat
clouds
angels
computer
pencil
wind
hands
breath
broom
peace
waiters
laughter
road
water
window

As you try to memorise the list, make up a story. An example of a story can be as follows:

I stood on a *chair* in my *house* to look out at a *tree* because there was a *book* on top of it. In the book was a *duck* swimming beside a *boat*. Above the boat there were *clouds* and *angels*. I was so surprised that I recorded all these in my *computer* instead of using my broken *pencil* which I had thrown to the *wind* with both my *hands* as I held my *breath*. A big *broom* came from

47

Mind-Body Power

nowhere and swept it away violently. This was followed by some *peace* until some *waiters* came, again as if from nowhere. They were filled with *laughter* as they came along on the *road*. I soon knew why when they poured *water* through my *window*.

By now you would have got an idea of what mental imaging is all about. The more creative you are in your visualisation, the better it is for whatever purpose you have set out to achieve. It is important to remember that the more suggestive links you can make in your visualisation exercises, the better you will remember and accelerate your learning.

REVISION EXERCISE

Taking a Trip

This is an exercise you can do daily to improve your visual skills and memory. This exercise is particularly good for people who have to commute every day.

When you are travelling from A to B, observe as much as you can — people, landmarks, signs, shops, colours, etc. After the trip, recall everything that you have seen by creative visualisation. Write these down. The next time you are on the same trip, check to see what you have got right and what you have missed. Continue doing this exercise until you have got every item down or until you are satisfied with your own progress.

If you like, you can vary this exercise by observing just one person while travelling in the train or bus. Don't stare but pick out the things about that person which tell a story. Does he look like a potential murderer? Is the dear old lady really a dear old lady? Or is she some kind of a witch behind the pleasant demeanour? Why does she always dress in black? Is she someone's grandmother or a lonely amah with no family? What is it about the people whom you are observing that gives you certain clues about their jobs, their characters, their lives?

Creative Visualisation

Of course, if you use this variation, you cannot really check if you are right, although if you are like me, you can. I usually find out in some way. That, I will leave to your imagination. Incidentally, this variation of the exercise is excellent for novelists, playwrights, detectives and anyone who needs to remember faces and people.

⊟ Accelerative Learning Programmes

An accelerative learning programme will only work if it is applied as an integrated system incorporating physical and mental relaxation and creative visualisation. This means that maximum results can only be achieved if you follow the programme systematically using the techniques which have been presented in the previous chapters. You should be careful not to miss or skip an element.

Having understood both the theoretical premises and the techniques of applying these principles, you are now ready to implement a programme of learning. Let us begin with learning a new language.

LEARNING A NEW LANGUAGE

Day 1

Select a piece of mood creating music from the music list in the appendix, eg, Steve Halpern's Study Suite. Put it on.

Next select a physical exercise from chapter 3, eg, Loving Myself. Do this for ten minutes.

After finishing your exercise, sit comfortably and prepare for breathing exercise. Do this for ten minutes or longer if you do not feel relaxed. You should only stop when you are relaxed. How do you know when you are relaxed? A good indication is that your eyelids have stopped flickering and your body feels like it is floating. Sometimes you may have the sensation that you are tilting over, rather like the falling sensation you have just before you fall asleep. Some people have also reported seeing flashing colours. If none of these happens, do not worry. You will know when you are relaxed. In this state of complete relaxation, begin creative visualisa-

50

Accelerative Learning Programmes

tion. Start with a goal setting exercise. Tell yourself:

- I want to learn French (or any other language you have chosen).
- Learning French is possible. It can be done.
- Learning French is easy.

As you say these things to yourself at this stage, really dwell on them. Go through each statement in your mind as if you are telling someone in your head. This is important because you are beginning to counter the logical-critical anti-suggestive barrier. This barrier if you remember occurs still on the conscious level. For instance, statements 1 and 2 may meet with no resistance. The third statement may encounter some resistance depending on your state of mind.

You may think that learning French is not easy because learning anything is hard work; it has always been for you. These are negative suggestions which have been fed into your conscious and unconscious minds. You must desuggest them away and replace them with positive suggestions. Say instead:

> Learning is easy when I am applying the techniques of accelerative learning. I have never used it before so I may as well give it a try. Nothing to lose but everything to gain. I'm going to be really fair to myself and give it a go.

Having convinced yourself on the conscious level, you can move on to the next step of goal setting visualisation.

Remember how to do it? Visualise now that you have mastered French. See yourself speaking French fluently. Make a movie in your mind — you are in Paris. It is springtime. You are walking along the left bank of the Seine, breathing in the freshness of spring. You smell crepes doused with Grand Marnier from a stall nearby, you see artists wearing berets standing in front of their easels painting. You stop behind one and watch his hand move deftly. He turns around. He smiles and says: 'Bonjour, Madame' and you say: 'Bonjour.' The French words roll off

51

Mind-Body Power

your tongue smoothly, easily. You continue to speak in French discussing the French impressionists.

Bear in mind the use of all your senses to visualise this scene. Let yourself really go into your feelings, in this case, exhiliration, joy, sense of achievement. Go through your body's sensations with each of these emotions. What is your heart doing? Is it pounding with exhiliration? Is your pulse rate racing with joy? Do your legs feel like jumping up and down with the sense of achievement?

After visualising the completion of your goal, think of something else deliberately to distract yourself from your set goal. If you have any doubts about your goal, they will enter your mind now. Let the doubts come in. And they will. *You are kidding yourself. Learning French is hard. Without a teacher especially. You are a dreamer. Forget it. Give it up. It's impossible.* WHATEVER HAPPENS AT THIS STAGE DO NOT GIVE IN TO YOUR DOUBTS. Do some fast talking and get rid of your doubts. Use every argument you can until the doubts disappear.

Having got rid of your doubts, you are on the way to success. So begin your planning. Still with your eyes closed and relaxed, systematically go through the reasons for wanting to learn French, then work out the various steps you need to take to achieve your goal, for example, designing a time-table for yourself, whether it be one hour or ten minutes put aside each day for studying new words. Picture it:

> You getting out of bed, brushing your teeth, having breakfast, going to your desk, opening your French book and reading the words for the time you have set yourself. Visualise the clock before you start and again when your elected time is up.

This rational planning while still in the relaxed meditative state ensures commitment and persistence on the unconscious level. To finish off, visualise all the things you can do once you have learnt French, that is, achieved your goal. You can talk to French artists on the left bank of the Seine, you can teach French, you can retire to the South of France.

52

Accelerative Learning Programmes

Tell yourself anything you like as long as you believe in them.
Count to four and open your eyes. Your unconscious is now set to work for you.

Learning The Materials

Creating suggestive effects

Give free rein to your inventiveness when creating suggestive effects for your learning programme. The space in which you are going to carry out your learning is crucial in terms of it having a suggestive effect on you. So create a suggestive atmosphere in the room where you are going to learn the materials. As this is a French lesson, you can do a bit of 'environmental manipulation' here by putting on your walls pictures of France or anything French. Hang a picture of Brigitte Bardot or Ives Montand on your wall. Scenic pictures of the Loire Valley where some of the best French wines come from can also create marvellous suggestive effects. These pictures act as a stimuli for your peripheral senses, in this instance, your sight.

For your audio sense, put on a piece of French music, eg *Frere Jacques*, to put you in a French mood.

Assume a different identity

This is a protective mechanism. By assuming a new identity, you suggest to yourself that it is all right to make mistakes so that you have more confidence and feel relaxed about learning a new language. Assume a French personality eg Napoleon or Brigitte Bardot. Believe in your new role. You are no longer you but Brigitte Bardot (or whoever you choose to be). This new role of yours becomes a psychologically protective personality.

Active concert

Put on a piece of classical music, eg Brahms' Concerto for

53

Mind-Body Power

Violin and Orchestra in D Major op. 77. (See appendix.)
With that as background music, read the materials to be
learnt, for example, the passage given below.

This could be a scene where you as Madame Bardot
converse with the immigration officer at the airport.

Immigration officer:	Votre passeport, s'il vous plait. (Your passport please.)
Madame Bardot:	Le voici, monsieur. (Here it is, sir.)
Immigration:	Combien le temps comptez-vous rester? (How long are you planning to stay?)
Madame Bardot:	Un mois, deux semaines, trois jours. (One month, two weeks, three days.)
Immigration:	Avez-vous quelque chose a declarer? (Have you anything to declare?)
Madame Bardot:	Excusez moi, je ne comprends pas. (Excuse me, I don't understand.)
Immigration:	Avez-vous quelque chose a declarer? (Have you got anything to declare?)
Madame Bardot:	Non, monsieur. (No, sir.)

Read the passage aloud. Dramatise the scene. When
reading the immigration officer's words, put on a grave voice,
deep tone and compose your face into that of his. Put yourself
into his role. When you are doing Madame Bardot, again act
the part. Do this in front of the mirror. It is more fun. This
stage is marvellous if you can get someone who knows
French to play the part of the immigration officer. Play acting
is introducing the fun element into your language learning.
When you are having fun, you continue to be relaxed which
is excellent for accelerating your learning process.

Pseudo passive concert

Select a piece of Baroque largo music. Put it on and while it is

54

Accelerative Learning Programmes

playing read the above passage again silently to yourself. Do not try too hard to remember the words or sentences. Just read it over once. What you are doing is giving unfocused attention to the materials and allowing your unconscious to take the materials in.

Practice

This is essentially the stage when you revise the materials already learnt. You can do this in many ways; it all depends on how much time you have to spare. One way is visualising the passage over in your mind when you are engaged in passive activities, for example, when you are commuting from A to B or when you are ironing. A very good time to go through the materials in your mind is just before you fall asleep: this enables your unconscious to do the revising for you when you are sleeping. Remember that your unconscious never sleeps. The first thing you should do on waking is recall the materials you have learnt the previous day.

Day 2

Learning A List Of New Words To Increase Vocabulary

Put on a piece of mood creating music and do your physical, breathing and mental exercises. Today, instead of a goal setting visualisation, do the early pleasant learning restimulation exercise (see chapter 4). With your eyes closed and the music playing, you are sitting very comfortably and letting your mind drift in and out of images.

Breathing normally, allow your images to take you back to the past when you were learning something. What is it? Learning to lick your first ice cream. You feel the sweet cool taste of ice cream on your tongue — smooth, sweet, cool — then it slides down your throat. You feel it trickling down your fingers so quickly that you lick and lick before it drips onto your clothing. It is good being able to lick the ice cream before it did that. It shows you are a smart kid. Learning to

Mind-Body Power

lick an ice cream is easy, really simple. You can do it with your eyes closed. You feel wonderful licking the ice cream as you play in the sun. Licking the ice cream is cool and nice. Learning is nice. Learning a new list of French words is nice just like licking the ice cream. It is fun and it is easy like eating the ice cream.

Slowly bring your mind back to the present and open your eyes. You are now ready to go on to the next lesson.

Review of day 1's lesson

Sit down with your note book and write down the whole passage. Having done that, go back and check how well you have done. If you have come to this stage of the book, you have done very well so anything you do now is a bonus. You are now ready for today's lesson.

We are going to learn some new words with you still as Madame Bardot. Today you are renting a car.
Here is a list of cars:
une voiture (one car)
une petite voiture (one small car)
une grande voiture (one big car)
une voiture de sport (one sports car)

Make a decision about which car you would like. Now tell the car rental man what you want eg 'I will have one sport's car' ('Je voudrais une voiture de sport').

Now that you have got your sports car, you drive to a restaurant. In the restaurant, you study the menu and then order the following:
(You already know how to say 'I'll have' — 'je voudrais'.)
du cafe (one coffee)
de l'eau chaude (some hot water)
du pain (some bread)
un oeuf sur le plat (one fried egg)
du bacon (some bacon)

56

Accelerative Learning Programmes

Associations

Now, in order to remember lesson 2, make up some associations of the words you have learnt today. For example, 'je' meaning 'I', you can say 'I' always come before 'J'. 'Voudrais' when read aloud sounds like the English word 'would' — that should make you think of the phrase 'I would like to have'.

By now you should have proved to yourself that learning French is easy. You feel fantastic and excited. You certainly feel more confident. As you continue with your French lessons, you will find that you will learn at a faster rate. At each progressive lesson, you will learn faster and faster. The learning amplification feedback system starts to operate — with a small input, the result is proportionately greater than the input, and then as you progressively increase the input, the result gets even greater and so on.

After having completed the two lessons, you should now continue with preparing materials for yourself. Below is a preparation guide.

Self Accelerative Learning Preparation Guide

Day of week: ....   Date ....

1. Statement of objective (what you are aiming to achieve, eg I want to master French in two months) ....
2. Physical exercise — 10 minutes
3. Mind calming exercise — 10 minutes
4. Suggestions to use (eg learning is easy, anyone can do it)
5. Creative visualisation, eg goal setting to be followed by early pleasant learning restimulation
6. Overview of materials to be learned
7. Music for pseudo passive concert — Baroque largo eg Vivaldi's *Winter*
8. Practice activity — association games, quiz, etc.
9. Self assessment for feedback
10. Revision — mental silent or aloud, etc.

Mind-Body Power

Aids To Your Self Accelerative Learning Programme

It helps if you can find a person who can do role playing with you, for instance, in the scene with the immigration officer, someone could take this role. Language is best learned with another person, as an element of fun can be introduced. The other person also provides dynamic interaction, and if he or she speaks the language you want to learn, it is even better. This is why a person learns a foreign language much faster if he or she lives in that country. These are of course ideal conditions.

Failing to find someone to do it with you, your next best recourse is a tape recorder. A double-decked tape recorder is a wonderful aid to your self accelerative learning programme. A set of language tapes is very useful. Put the active concert tape in one deck and the pseudo passive concert music tape in the other.

LEARNING PHYSICAL SKILLS

Learning How Yo Swim

Although swimming is a physical skill, it requires the same mental programme. The following programme is set out with the assumption that you do want to learn swimming and are not forced into it. If this is the case, then it is very easy, and takes no time at all to learn.

You have to set up a mental programme for yourself similar to the one used for learning a language. Setting the atmosphere with music, and physical and breathing exercises are followed by goal setting. Include early pleasant learning restimulation if you like. In addition, do the following visualisation exercise to music.

Visualisation for learning to swim

- Imagine yourself in a swimming position, that is, lift both arms above your head, bend your body slightly as if to dive

Accelerative Learning Programmes

into the water.
- Move your arms in swimming strokes — overarm strokes — left, right, left, right. Accompany this with the appropriate rhythmic breathing.
- As you get the feel of the swimming movements, feel the water swish over your body, hear the sound of your breathing, smell the briny salt (or chlorine if you are swimming in a pool) and enjoy the total experience.

Now go for your swimming lesson and do what you have accomplished in your mind. Watching other good swimmers helps in making your visualisation more vivid so do watch other swimmers whenever you have the opportunity.

For those who are afraid of water

As someone who loves water, I always feel so sad for people who would like to swim but at the same time are terrified of putting their heads in the water. They fear their heads being submerged. This is a mild phobia for many people. It is not really the fear of drowning. It is the fear of the sensation of being submerged, losing control. A lot of us have fears — fear of letting go, fear of ridicule, fear that no one will love us, and so on. Of all the human emotions known to man, the most terrible is fear and the most miraculous is love. Until we get rid of fear, our learning and most probably our lives will not be very fulfilling. In this case when a person fears being submerged in water yet loves the idea of knowing how to swim, the solution is simple. You must find a way to make your love for swimming outstrip the fear of losing control and of being submerged. The following programme should be adhered to strictly in sequence.

- Physical exercise — at least half an hour devoted to some kind of aerobic exercises, eg, brisk walking, running, skipping and dancing, that gets your heart rate going. For people who have never done any strenuous exercise before please check with your doctor prior to this.

59

Mind-Body Power

- After this exercise, have a shower or bath. Accompany it with Baroque music. Say to yourself that water soothes and is pleasant. This is an important step. While having your bath or shower, make some effort to splash water on your face. Then cup water in your hands and dip your face in. If you feel frightened doing this, do some rhythmic breathing before you dip your face in. Gradually leave your face longer in the water as your fear lessens. Do deep rhythmic breathing to counteract physical signs of anxiety such as heart thumping after each dip.

- After the shower, continue with deep relaxation breathing accompanied by Baroque music. Make sure your posture is very comfortable either sitting down or lying flat on the floor. Don't fall asleep. Repeat to yourself that water is soothing and pleasant.

- Do a visualisation exercise on loving water. Go through the sensations of being under the shower again in your mind, enjoying the water running down your body. Visualise your face dipped in your cupped hands. Nothing terrible happened, did it? You are now sitting relaxed and happy, safe and sound. Go deep into your feelings of security. Let yourself feel secure, while doing this exercise.

- Follow this with a goal setting visualisation exercise (see chapter 4).

- Go for your swim after this.

A final hint is try to swim with someone you love and have lots of fun with, and who can make you laugh. Don't learn to swim consciously but play around in the water. Laugh. Be a child again. Children learn while they are playing. So can you.

LEARNING TO UNLEARN A BAD HABIT

Learning To Give Up Smoking

The only good thing about bad habits is that they are learned

60

Accelerative Learning Programmes

and so they can be unlearned. Smoking is one of these bad habits, and more serious than other habits because it is also a physical addiction. Even so, smoking can be unlearned. It depends on whether or not you want to. I was a smoker for 20 years and am now no longer one. I unlearned the habit by applying the principles of accelerative learning. You can do it too.

Habitual smoking for a long period of time has reasons deeply embedded in the unconscious and the conscious. The conscious reason smokers give as to why they do not give it up is that they enjoy it. They find it pleasurable. Then there are those who do not know on a conscious level that they need it for all kinds of reasons, eg security, or to feel glamourous.

To learn how to give up smoking requires an attack on both fronts — the conscious and the unconscious. The first step is to recognise the reasons on a conscious level as to why you smoke.

On the conscious level

- Take out a piece of paper and write down how you took up smoking, eg your friends smoked at parties and they offered you some cigarettes. You had continued to smoke at parties or when with friends in a social situations.

  Now write down the reasons as to why you STILL smoke. Be very honest. No one is going to see what you have written. It is nobody's business except your own.

- Examine what you have written and see what the associations are. For example, do you smoke only in social situations now? Continue to work out as many associations as you can. Working out the associations, that is, the reasons you smoke now and their connections with the reasons you took up smoking in the beginning, will enable you to view the situation with your logical-critical faculty on a conscious level. What can you find out by examining what you have written? You will discover the situations in which you need a cigarette most. For example, if you had taken up smoking because of social reasons, then it is most

Mind-Body Power

likely parties are 'at risk' occasions for you when you are trying to give up smoking, so they are to be avoided as much as possible during the period of your unlearning how to smoke. At least until you are no longer as vulnerable.

- Now make a fresh list in a table as shown below. The first column lists all the situations in which you desperately need to smoke. The second indicates whether or not these situations can be avoided, eg you need to smoke in the office but you cannot avoid going to work, can you? If a situation can be avoided, then state how under this second column, eg if you need to smoke when watching tv, you can avoid the situation by not watching tv, and doing something else instead, such as reading in bed, when you do not feel a compulsion to smoke. Remember to list only the situations in which you simply cannot do without a cigarette. What we are doing here is try and break the associative link between your smoking and the activity, event or occasion which induces you to smoke.

Situation most vulnerable	Can it be avoided?
working in office	no
watching tv at home	yes, don't watch tv

- Write down all the reasons you want to give up smoking.

The unconscious level

- Do aerobic exercise for half an hour eg brisk walking, jogging, swimming, gymnastics, etc. Please consult your doctor before engaging in strenuous exercises if you have not exercised for a long time.

- Put on Baroque music and do deep rhythmic breathing until very relaxed.

- Do the creative goal setting exercise. Set your goal in the affirmative eg — *I want to give up smoking, I want to be a nonsmoker. I can give up smoking*. Be realistic about your

Accelerative Learning Programmes

step by step plans. For example, do not give up smoking and eating your favourite foods at the same time. Take it step by step. If you smoke two packets a day, cut down to one a day, then half, then a quarter. At the stage when doubts pour in, think of the reasons you have written down previously and counteract your doubts with them. Be very meticulous about visualising your plan on how to go about putting your campaign into operation. Once the desire to give up smoking reaches your unconscious, then it is easy. You will find that you do want to give up smoking.

• Implement steps 1 and 3 daily for a few weeks and if you haven't smoked all this time, change your goal to 'I will never smoke again'. Chant this over again and again during your daily visualisation exercise.

• After not smoking for a few months, and your health is much better and you are happier, don't forget to implement the above creative visualisation exercise every now and then just to remind your unconscious. Say the following: 'I thank myself for the power within me to give up smoking. I will never smoke again.'

The better you know yourself, the stronger are your convictions and suggestions to your unconscious. What do I mean by that? When I decided to give up smoking, I knew that I couldn't do it for health reasons for cancer doesn't frighten me and death doesn't frighten me. Lots of people are like that. Fear of death does not really motivate people into changing their behaviour. Otherwise people won't smoke, drink, fly in planes and drive cars, and more recently in light of the AIDS scare, have random sex partners. As I am not afraid of death it was no use, as far as I was concerned, reading literature on cancer and smoking. Cancer was something that happened to other people and not to me. I believed myself to be invincible and even if I didn't, at heart I am a fatalist. Death is death. One cannot prevent it. Such was my thinking both consciously and unconsciously that I simply couldn't give up smoking using the health argument.

Mind-Body Power

However, the desire to give up smoking was there. At first it was only a conscious decision — a logical, intellectual one. Nothing happened. For months I toyed with the idea and for months I continued smoking and enjoying it, telling myself that if I really wanted to I could. How many of you have said that? Until one day when as usual I started the day with a jog and a swim, then a shower. This was followed by an hour of yoga. After that, I went to my study and lit a cigarette as I sat down to work.

Something clicked at that moment. I saw myself for what I was. A hypocrite. Here I was doing all the wonderfully healthy things — and then lighting a cigarette. It was the contradiction in my behaviour and the fact that I was being hypocritical which I could not tolerate. I could not live with that. No one knew about that but it was enough that I knew. I put out that cigarette and have never smoked again since.

That is what I mean by knowing yourself well. Figure out what drives you, what you cannot live with, what sort of things you can give up and what you cannot. Work out the associative and suggestive links with the idea of giving up smoking.

Some Do's and Don'ts

Do

- seek support from people who love and support you and who won't criticise
- love yourself and pamper yourself because you are doing something marvellous
- be kind to yourself
- have plenty of rest and sleep
- trust yourself
- think positive

Accelerative Learning Programmes

Don't

- associate with people who ridicule and jeer your efforts
- overwork
- make big changes in your life
- give up other addictions at the same time. If you start and give up, start and give up, don't lose heart. At least you have started. That's what counts and as long as you keep starting, there is still hope that you will eventually give up smoking altogether.

UNLEARNING A PSYCHOLOGICAL ADDICTION

More than physical addiction, what is truly amazing is our ability to be addicted to certain patterns of behaviour which we do not think are addictive. Yet these patterns of behaviour could be addictive and may present as problems. These patterns of behaviour could simply be patterns of thinking or they could be overt behavioural patterns. For instance, I know of a woman who thinks that she is awful. It does not matter what she does, she will come out with the statement: 'I am awful.' Even after a brilliantly prepared meal, she would still say that she was awful to have prepared such an awful meal. She is not pretending but believes in all sincerity that she has not done well. And nothing could shift her from this opinion of herself. The consequence of this is that she cannot realise her full potential. Such patterns of thinking are addictive. And destructive.

Covert patterns of behaviour which are addictive can be seen in people who cannot say no when they are asked to do something for someone. This is in spite of not having enough time or it may be overly stressful to herself. For instance, there are women and men who say yes to every request that is made to them — cook for the school fete, sit on a church committee, chauffeur little Johnny and his friends to the school dance and so on. All this 'yessing' besides a fulltime job and being a fulltime parent and spouse. Asking for a

65

Mind-Body Power

nervous breakdown? Yes.

One of my mature female students often bemoans this problem to me. She is cooking for every school fete and chauffeuring every old lady and child in the neighbourhood to everything that is going on. Such a cycle of 'I must do it or else no one would' needs to be broken, yet often people who are caught in it find difficulty in doing so. One of the reasons for this is that such people have formed an addiction of saying yes. This is a psychological addiction. As such it can be broken by applying accelerative learning principles to un-learn such a bad habit.

Again this has to be confronted on both the conscious and the unconscious levels. Once you have identified a particular habit of yours which you see as problematic, then you have to combat it on a conscious level first. The following is a programme that you can use on a conscious level:

- State the problem either verbally or write it down.

- State the reasons why it is a problem eg it stops you from getting a promotion or you are wasting too much time.

- State the positive consequences of getting rid of this addictive habit eg increased self confidence, self esteem.

For confronting the problem on an unconscious level, implement your accelerative learning programme using physical exercise, mental exercise, music and creative visualisation to desuggest-suggest materials in yourself. For example, after doing your exercises, settle down to some creative visualisation, see yourself as a very self controlled person who can command his own actions. See in your mind's eye the power of a person who is very good in this eg either Jesus Christ if you are brought up in the tradition of Christianity or Buddha if you are a Buddhist. Both figures have a reputation for self discipline. This is of course important associative and suggestive linkages. To undo an addiction requires will power and self discipline. You can choose anyone you like. I, for instance, choose the figure of a beloved teacher who was influential in my education.

66

Accelerative Learning Programmes

Picture a scene of relaxation, eg a walk in the forest. Walk towards this figure of your choice. From afar, you can see his approaching figure. As the two of you walk towards each other, you can hear the singing of birds, the sound of music, and soft breezes caress your cheek. You feel happy and relaxed. Joy abounds in your heart as you walk to meet this person coming towards you. As the two of you meet, you melt into the person and BECOME the person. As you become this person, say to yourself, it is possible to give up saying yes.

In this chapter you have learnt to design a variety of accelerative learning programmes for different types of skills. The subject matter of your learning as you have seen does not matter — it can be a verbal skill as in learning a language; it can be a physical skill as in learning how to swim; it can be learning to unlearn a bad habit. It is the process of learning that is important. This you have learnt. Now it is up to you to apply it, extend it and extrapolate from it for anything you wish to learn. Be creative and adventurous.

⊟ Teaching Others — You As Teacher

We must first learn how to learn, then only can we teach. There is a student and a teacher in all of us. The principles of accelerative learning that we use to teach ourselves can now be applied to the teaching of others whether they are our own children or they are our students, in a formal classroom situation. Of course, it applies to any teaching, even something as informal as teaching a friend to sing a song.

Many of the elements already discussed in the previous chapters of this book are applicable to the teaching of others. However, a number of things can be included, particularly in the area of suggestion and the type of teacher you should be. When combined carefully and creatively the suggestions you use and the type of teacher you are to your students are indeed a powerful combination. For this reason it is important to know what types of suggestion are applicable and what kind of teacher qualities should be cultivated in programmes which use accelerative teaching and learning.

THE TEACHER

The teacher is a very important person in accelerative teaching — what he thinks and feels, and how these are communicated verbally and nonverbally. Everything you do is communicated to the student either consciously or unconsciously. It does not matter whether the student is a two year old toddler or a final year university student. When you teach, you must teach with love and understanding, empathy and creativity, enthusiasm and joy. Unless you do so, accelerative learning in your students will not take place. As every teacher knows, it is hard to be enthusiastic about a subject that you dislike teaching, and facing students whom

68

Teaching Others — You As Teacher

you do not like.

Lozanov suggests the following principles which teachers can use to initiate and maintain accelerative learning in their students:

- Authority — the teacher must know his subject very well and know how to teach it.

- The teacher must bring about a childlike open curious state and/or mood in the students. Learning is a natural state of the human being and nowhere is this more apparent than at the infant stage when we learn our mother tongue.

  The teacher must have the ability to take his students back to that stage again when learning is spontaneously joyous, effortless, playful and, for most the time, done unconsciously. Infants learn without knowing that they are doing so. Imagination is stimulated, the powers lying in the mind are released.

  As a teacher, when you can bring about this state of infantilisation in your students during the learning process, you have come close to performing a miracle. When your students are in this state, accelerative learning takes place.

- The teacher must know how to use double planeness. This is communication directed at the conscious and unconscious minds of the student. Double planeness refers to the 'how' rather than the 'what' of being taught. How you say something is important in terms of it being absorbed and remembered by your students.

- The teacher uses intonation creatively and dynamically. The information is communicated in a dramatic way to facilitate absorption and retention.

- The use of music to simulate concerts so students can absorb information the way an audience at a concert does — passive, yet alert and interested. In this way, Lozanov claims, infomation can be absorbed without apparent effort. It is what Lozanov calls a pseudo passive concert review. It refers to the situation when a person goes to a concert of his favourite composers. His attitude is

69

Mind-Body Power

one of expectancy and anticipation of being entertained, of going to something enjoyable and relaxing. The teacher uses the pseudo passive concert by creating the same expectancy thus getting a whole group of people to concentrate at the same time. (See chapter 3.)

All these principles must be thought through carefully before you begin your lesson. None of them can be ranked as more important than the others; they should be used as an integrated whole regardless of the subject matter to be taught. You can begin with one method, and as the students' learning pattern begins to change slowly, you add another one. Continue doing this as the rate of change in the students increases. Essentially this creates the learning amplification feedback system — what Donald Schuster and Charles Gritton called the snowball effect (1985).

TYPES OF SUGGESTIONS TO USE

In teaching someone else to learn acceleratively, the teacher has a vast repertoire of suggestions that he can use. These are very important as according to our communications model presented in chapter 2, we have seen that when a person is in a state of relaxation, suggestions can be fed in more easily. If suggestions are not rejected by the anti-suggestive barriers, they are taken into our unconscious. Once absorbed into our unconscious, these suggestions begin their powerful work to bring about results undreamt of. We develop better memory and learn with greater speed and understanding.

Suggestions work in the form of expectancies given by you to your student. For example, you can say: 'If you study very hard, I expect that you will pass with high distinctions.' In saying this, you have communicated directly to your student an expectancy on your part. Every day in our lives we use such direct suggestions and these work on our recipients sometimes without them being aware of it. Remember that suggestion is a constant factor in all communication as I have pointed out in chapter 2.

70

Teaching Others — You As Teacher

One of the strongest suggestive factors in my early academic career was my father's expectation that I would perform to the best of my ability and achieve whatever I set out to do. It was a suggestion that was never stated explicitly yet like all children, I knew intuitively that that was my father's expectation of me. And because I also knew that my father loved me and believed in me, I grew up believing in myself. As such, my father had given the greatest gift any parent can give to his child — self esteem and a belief in oneself. Teachers should be able to give their students this. If through your suggestions, direct and indirect, if through your teaching, your student or child can learn to believe in himself and his own ability, you have imparted what is tantamount to one of the greatest gifts any human being can give to another. The suggestions you use as a teacher must therefore be absolutely full of integrity, and uppermost in your mind should be the welfare of your students when making these suggestions.

There are many different expressions of suggestions. Suggestions can take the form of verbal and nonverbal expressions, and work best when they break down the anti-suggestive barriers and enter the unconscious. Sometimes they can work on the conscious mind as well.

Direct Verbal Suggestions*

The most common suggestions are those which are direct and aim at the student's consciousness, eg saying that learning is as easy as ABC. Direct verbal suggestions work best on children because they have not developed their logical-critical faculty. They still operate on the level of their intuition and emotion. For an adult student, direct verbal suggestions have to confront the three anti-suggestive barriers explained in chapter 2. For example, the student's logical-critical faculty on a conscious level can present very strong arguments to

* This section on the different types of suggestions is adapted from Donald Schuster and Charles E. Gritton, *Manual on Suggestive Accelerative Learning Techniques*, 1985.

71

Mind-Body Power

reject the idea that learning is easy. I remember once when a new teacher told me that a particular mathematics lesson was easy and immediately I responded by saying that it was hard. The teacher did not argue. How could he in the face of such strong conviction? If he had and then showed how easy it was, he would have convinced me on logical grounds. Who knows — I could have been a brilliant mathematician today instead of a social scientist.

Indirect Verbal Suggestion

Indirect verbal suggestions are more subtle and confront the unconscious more cleverly than direct verbal suggestions. There are many different examples of indirect verbal suggestions.

Truisms

These are statements which are self evident truths. Usually for most of us the self evident truth of such statements has been validated by past experience so often that they cannot be possibly anything else but true. For example, the following statements are truisms:

- Some people learn faster than others.

- You will learn more easily when you are ready for it.

It is important when you are using this form of suggestion that you include a deadline, eg:

> You will learn easily when you are ready after three days of preparatory work on accelerative principles.

Simple binds

Simple binding is the posing of two alternatives which leads to the same result or outcome. An example of a simple bind is a situation in which a child refuses to go to sleep and is asked if he would like to sleep in his parents' room or in his own cot. It is like asking the question: 'Do you want to learn

Teaching Others — You As Teacher

quickly or slowly?'

Either answer gets to the goal of learning.

Focusing questions

These are questions which cannot be answered or responded to by the conscious mind. When you give these questions to your students, they have to rely on their imagination to formulate a response. For example, in a physics lesson you can ask the following question:

Can you imagine that you are Albert Einstein poring over his books in today's physics lesson?

Yes sets

This is a set of questions which calls for an obvious 'yes' for answer to every question, with the final one being the suggestion required by you, the teacher.
Example:

Today is a geography lesson, right? We are going to study the capital cities of Malaysia now, are we not? Will you find that easy?

Compound suggestions

A compound suggestion consists of two statements which are connected by the conjunction 'and'. The first is a truism and the second is a suggestion. For example, a teacher may say to the class:

—We have completed all our lessons for this term earlier than usual (and) now I want you to learn next term's work at a faster rate which I am sure all of you can do easily.

OR

—You are sitting here quietly now (and) that makes it easier for us to memorise many new words today.

73

Mind-Body Power

OR

—All of us have an enormous reserve capacity (and) we can tap it in today's competition by winning.

Double binds

These are questions which cannot be resolved by a student's conscious mind. For example, a series of questions can be posed like the following:

> Your body is relaxed now as you listen to the music. I want you to think about what makes you feel more joyous — the feeling of a warm relaxed body or the feeling that your mind is crystal clear and you can see everything sharply?

Your student will face a dilemma if he tries to answer this by using his conscious mind because he likes both. Both are equally good or bad. It is rather like asking a child who she can do without — mummy or daddy. It is a no win situation. Given such a dilemma, the student will resort to his unconscious mind to find an answer. In this sense, double binds are more complex than simple binds and should be carefully phrased at all times if you are going to use them.

Complex contingent suggestion

This indirect verbal suggestion has a particular formula. You can·begin with a negative, puzzling, and ambiguous statement. Follow this statement with a suggestion. While your student's conscious mind is busy processing the first statement which should be deliberately designed to require more conscious attention to unravel, you slot in the suggestion. For example:

—Don't bother using your mind to concentrate on what I am saying until (you are relaxed).

—Don't worry about passing the tests until (you find yourself learning very easily).

Teaching Others — You As Teacher

The statements in parentheses are the suggestions.

Complex contingent suggestions can be made more powerful if they are said with tonal variation. For example, you can say in your normal tone 'Don't worry', then in a louder tone, say 'about passing the tests', and conclude in your normal tone with the suggestion in parentheses.

Direct Nonverbal Suggestion

Direct nonverbal suggestions are the bread and butter of good actors and actresses for essentially these are mime, that is, acting without words. In its simplest form it is the child's imitation of mum and dad and others. An occasion where a direct nonverbal suggestion was given to me was when I had lunch for the first time at a girls' hostel upon my arrival in Australia. I did not know what the rules and regulations were. When I entered the dining room, everyone was already seated and drinking their soup. The hall was dead quiet. Right through the meal no one spoke at the table. The direct nonverbal suggestion was very powerful as I found out later. No one was to speak until dessert was served. Neither did I speak at meal times for the three months that I stayed at the hostel. To this day whenever I have to sit in a hostel dining room, I feel a compulsion to eat silently.

Indirect Nonverbal Suggestions

Body language

When you want to make indirect nonverbal suggestions, you have to rely on body language. Facial expressions are very effective in conveying nonverbal suggestions. For example, how you walk into your classroom — are you dragging your feet, head down or do you bounce into the room, head erect with a smile on your face? I have tried it out on my students. When I walk into the classroom looking gloomy, the students look tired and dull. When I bounce into the room, plonk my

75

Mind-Body Power

things down on the desk and look at them with a lively expression, they sit up and pay more attention for the lessons.

Feelings are conveyed in your tone. If you talk excitely about the weather, your tone, not your words suggest that there is something exciting about the weather. When I was taking drama lessons as a student, one of the exercises we had to do was to say a statement several times, each time expressing a different emotion.

Suggestions are also carried via your eyes. Your eyes are indeed the mirrors of your soul. The glare can be a powerful deterrent in disciplining a child and the smile a satisfying reward. Eye contact is extremely important in conveying suggestions. You as a teacher can use it to hold the attention of your students. Holding eye contact with your student also suggests to him that you are requiring his attention.

Environmental suggestions

Rearranging the environment is another way of creating indirect nonverbal suggestions. By setting up the physical space be it a classroom or any other location used for your teaching, you can bring about suggestive effects. For instance, I always do my yoga session in the same spot of one room in the house. The mere act of being in the room brings about a relaxed calm state in me. Teachers can create suggestive effects by decorating their classrooms appropriately. Making use of lighting and colours is a very effective way of influencing moods. Our sense of smell is also important so the burning incense or having fragrant flowers in a room can bring about the suggestive effect you want.

Environmental arrangements as a form of nonverbal indirect suggestion gives you plenty of room to be creative. Its possibilities are limitless as most conscientious teachers know.

Teaching Others — You As Teacher

SOME DO'S AND DONT'S WHEN TEACHING

- Don't use criticisms eg 'What's the matter with you? Are you stupid or something?' Beware of criticisms which are unspoken but conveyed by your body language and tone of voice. Impatience can be easily detected even in a very controlled voice. This is easily picked up even by small children. In fact, children are very intuitive and, although unable or reluctant to challenge the teacher, once they sense impatience or anger in you, their anxiety becomes a block to their learning. So the more you display negative emotions, the worse it is for the learning process.

- Never, never put down a student, embarrass or use sarcasm on the student. Never say: 'You are wrong.'

- Don't pick on a student. Don't wait too long for a response to a question without giving it tactfully. Ten to 15 seconds' wait is long enough. Make question time a fun activity rather than an interrogation. I have gone round the class with questions put to every student in the form of a game. That relaxes them and they don't mind when they can't give an answer or give a wrong answer. Later on, you can repeat the correct answer without drawing any attention to it or cause any embarrassment to the student. Avoid overcorrection, punishment, quiet warnings and negative reinforcement.

- Remember that your student is a human being and in that sense, he or she is your peer. You can give your student a part to play as a protective shield. For example, when studying a Shakespeare play, say *Hamlet*, a student can be Hamlet, another can be Ophelia and so on until the whole play is read for the term or whatever time is set. So when Hamlet forgets his lines, it does not matter to the student, he or she is not committing the mistakes. Always protect the self image of the student, jsut as yours needs to be protected.

  When you are teaching your child the multiplication tables, you can say to him that he is Mr Multi, not your son, for the time he and you are learning the multiplication

77

Mind-Body Power

tables. Be inventive, playful and creative, and the student learns faster and better.

- The teacher should be an actor and you are if you are standing in front of the class. Your job is to communicate something, that is, teach something. This can be anything, from simple information to complex emotions, from simply describing a scene from history to explaining where babies come from to a four year old. As an actor you should be entertaining as well. You should amuse and never bore as you teach. You dramatise whenever possible, in verbal and nonverbal language. Your voice and tone, your facial expressions and your body movement are all tools for dramatisation of a lesson. The more dynamic and dramatic you are, the better the lesson will be learnt by your student.

- Believe in yourself, your teaching ability and the subject matter that is being taught, and believe in your students. You must, as a teacher, convey to your students that what you are doing is worth doing. It is not just a job.

- Be happy in what you are teaching. Put on a happy smile. This is a tall order, you may think, because who can be happy in a hot, stuffy classroom? Who can be happy all the time when students don't want to learn? How can you be happy, you may groan, when you are pitting yourself against a system you didn't create in the first place?

  If you think like that, then you had better do something about those thoughts if you are to continue teaching effectively. If you are discouraged at times, pretend that you are happy, put on a smile as you walk into the classroom. In other words, be a good actor. You may find to your pleasant surprise that your students respond. People usually do. Try it.

HOW TO PREPARE A LESSON

An accelerative teaching session involves three major stages, namely, preparation, presentation and practice.

78

Teaching Others — You As Teacher

Preparation

Prepare the physical environment in which the lesson will take place. Is it clean and comfortable? What is the level of noise and interference from outside? Is it appealing to the eyes? Is it suggestive of relaxation? What other suggestive effects are to be created? Arrange chairs and other furniture to foster a relaxed atmosphere, for example, in a circular format rather than students sitting one row behind another with teacher at the front.

Prepare the materials for your lesson. Be clear about the objectives of that particular lesson. Is it to teach the students analytical skills? Is the lesson merely informative and students are required to memorise facts and figures? Unless you are clear about the objectives you seek to achieve, you cannot expect your students to be. Select physical and mental relaxation exercises to be used for the lesson. When doing this, bear in mind the time and space limits. If you are going to have 20 students in a small room, then select an exercise which does not require so much room.

Select two pieces of music, one for the active concert and one for the pseudo passive concert (see appendix).

Practise the suggestions that you want to use no matter how simple they are eg truisms, simple binds, and so on.

Prepare yourself — by this I refer to your mental set. Get rid of negative thoughts by creative imaging.

Presentation

This phase of the lesson should begin with an overview of what the lesson's objective is. Tell your students what you are going to teach them, what for, how this lesson's materials fit in with what they have done in the previous lesson and how it will prepare them for the following lesson. For example, in an English lesson you may say something like this:

We are going to learn sentence construction in today's lesson . This is progressing from the 100 new words you

79

Mind-Body Power

have learnt yesterday. After today's lesson, you will be able to write a short composition in our next lesson.

Do physical relaxation exercise. This takes about 5 minutes depending on how much time you have. This is to be followed by breathing exercise. Five minutes of this will be sufficient. Then 5 minutes of mind calming exercise follows. When your students are relaxed, do the goal setting exercise with them (see chapter 4). This takes another 5 minutes. Make some positive suggestions to get rid of their negative blocks to learning. Alternatively, if time allows, use creative visualisation techniques, eg early pleasant learning restimulation (see chapter 4).

Active concert

When you are certain that everyone is ready, put on classical music and present the lesson's materials dramatically. This could be done by varying your tone, increasing and decreasing the volume of your voice and, if you are able to, whenever possible, dramatise with gestures. Every teacher who wants to use the accelerative teaching method must learn how to dramatise.

At this stage, everything that you are as an actor — dramatic and dynamic, interesting and entertaining — must be put into use. The classical music and your dramatisation of the lesson's materials serve the purpose of stimulating the students' imagination. This enables them to produce visual imagery and associations. For example, if you are conducting a lesson of the rivers in Malaysia, *Rasa Sayang* can be played in the background.

Dramatic presentation includes intonation. This is perhaps one of the most satisfying aspects of teaching for it is here that all your performing talents can come to the fore — your voice is one of the most powerful tools you have as a teacher. Remember the four d's — deliberate, dramatic, dynamic delivery is the key to success. There are a variety of ways to do this. You can use a cycle of normal tone followed by loud and then soft: 'This is the Perak River and THAT IS THE

Teaching Others — You As Teacher

KLANG RIVER and over there is the Kinta River (soft).'
Convey emotions in your voice. Use your tone and pitch
differently rather than engage in a monotone. Read the text
with your voice louder than the music or at least at the same
volume. Ask the students to follow the text silently with their
eyes as you read.

Pseudo passive concert

Put on a Baroque largo piece from your selection. This is an
important stage in terms of accelerative learning as the
students now learn without apparent effort. The students are
flowing with the music and letting images come and go in
their minds. They are asked to defocus and not to actively
work in trying to remember the materials to be learnt. They
should have their eyes shut during the pseudo passive concert
session.

Practice

Conventional as it may seem, practice is extremely crucial in
the form of feedback. People learn better when they know
their own progress. This is conventional education wisdom.
Similarly in accelerative teaching, students must be shown the
fact that they have learnt. Again a number of ways are
possible to demonstrate this.

● *Activation* — students are asked to do something with
what they have learnt. If you have just taught them a
lesson in numbers, then ask them to enact a shopping scene
in which they have to count the change. In a language
class, a sing-along is always very successful and enjoyable.
If students have just learnt the names of flora and fauna of
the Amazon jungle, take them on a mental trip; different
animal roles can be assumed by the students. In a sociology
class on organisations, I have asked students to role-play
characters in a particular company or bureaucracy and,
believe me, they enjoy it more than sitting through a
tutorial paper on Weber's ideal type of bureacracy.

Mind-Body Power

- *Elaboration* — the concepts or materials learnt are elaborated in different ways by the students. They can be elaborated in the form of a skit, a play, a video or any other practical project. For example, in a foreign language class, students can be taken to the local market to bargain for things. This was done in Australia with migrants learning English. In countries where it is not possible or practical to do this, an expatriate association or club can be used instead. For instance, if German is being taught, the teacher can organise a luncheon between students and club members.

  Games in which groups of students pit themselves against each other in an atmosphere of camaraderie are also excellent. In a sociology class I divided the class into three groups of eight with each group assuming the persona of a major theorist. One group was Talcott Parsons, another group was Karl Marx and another group was George Herbert Mead. All three have differences in their theoretical orientations so the students had a ball elaborating and applying their ideas.

- *Tests* — ultimately any system of feedback is the test. The type of test can vary from a quiz to a self correction test. A grade can be given to a monthly or termly examination but tests and quizzes serve the function of practice in a very crucial way.

  Be very clear about what you are testing and measuring in your test and inform your students accordingly. If it is just testing their memory, then say so. If it is analytical skills you are testing, tell them so.

  Be creative in the types of tests you set. Tests do not have to be a question-answer type necessarily. For example, in a third year sociology course on ageing, I set a test in which the students have to ask ten questions. I told them that they would be assessed on the conceptual and theoretical understanding of the topic. So in a sense these questions are summarised critiques of various aspects of the topic.

  Why can't students be assessed as a group? Why shouldn't students assess themselves in terms of time and

Teaching Others — You As Teacher

effort they put into a project? In Literature, tests can take the form of a short skit, a scene from a particular novel.

Assessment and the giving of grades can be unconventional too. It is important to remember that a student is assessed on how much he has learnt and not how well he can fail. The job as a teacher is not to fail but to pass the students. It is always sad when I see the surprise on the students' faces when I tell them this because they are so conditioned to believe otherwise after being told implicitly and explicitly that teachers are there to make life difficult for them and their primary task as students is to beat the system and get by without failing.

The three stages of teaching a class are preparation, presentation and practice. These three stages can be broken down into several sub stages, each to be carefully linked to the other.

After giving your students the required number of lessons, be it history, sex education, swimming or reading, the time will come when your role is to step back as a teacher and let your students take over their own learning. Your task is completed when you have taught your students how to learn. In doing so, you have taught them how to teach themselves. And if they love doing both, you have achieved much.

TEACHING A FRIEND ELEMENTARY CHINESE CHARACTERS

Not all of us are teachers in a classroom. Often, we are required to teach a friend something, so it is useful to know that by applying accelerative teaching techniques we can impart our knowledge and skill to our friends in an enjoyable manner. In this section, we are going to teach a friend how to read and write some simple Chinese characters.

83

Mind-Body Power

Preparation

Find a place where both you and your friend are comfortable in, preferably with no interruption from people and noise. It is important that you use the same place for every lesson since your friend must associate the room with learning Chinese. More importantly he must also associate the room with you in it as his teacher and not a friend. Unless he accepts you in your role as his teacher, teaching him will be difficult. Similarly you must accept him as your student and no longer your friend. In short, in this room where you have chosen to be your 'classroom' both you and your friend begin to role play, that is, both of you assume new roles, as teacher and student.

You will need to prepare your materials for your lesson. Decide what words you want to teach and write these on large pieces of paper such as mahjong paper (approximately 865mm by 865mm). So, for example, if you decide for lesson one you wish to teach 16 characters, then each of these should be written on a piece of mahjong paper. Stick these on the walls in the room where the lesson is to be held.

Select some quiet Chinese melodies without lyrics for mood music. This should be playing in the room at the beginning of the lesson. At every lesson, the same music should be played as you start your lesson. This is to create a suggestive link between the place and the Chinese lesson to be conducted. The same music acts very much like a 'signature tune' so each time your friend hears the tune, he is mentally prepared for his Chinese lesson. Also select a piece of music for the active concert and a Baroque largo piece for the pseudo passive concert. These pieces can vary from lesson to lesson.

Presentation

Physical and breathing exercises

While the mood music is playing, begin the lesson with five

Teaching Others — You As Teacher

minutes of physical exercise (see chapter 3) and five minutes of breathing exercise to get your friend relaxed.

Creative visualisation

With the selected mood music still playing, take your friend through the early pleasant learning restimulation exercise (see chapter 4). Begin by telling your friend to find an instance in his life when he was learning something pleasant. Make suggestions such as: 'Do you remember the first time you read a good book and learn something from it?' It is important that you make him understand what he is to think of so suggestions are important, but not too many at once. If he is not a reader, suggest a movie, and so on. The start of pleasant learning restimulation is very important. If you confuse him, or he is not clear as to what is required, then you break his relaxed mood. Remember that it must be something that he has enjoyed doing, not simply the achievement of it (see chapter 4).

Use the following as a guide for this lesson: 'Now that you have found a learning situation that you are enjoying, what are you doing? Where are you? Who is around you? What can you see? What can you hear? what can you smell? What can you feel? Be aware of your feelings of joy and pleasure.'

'Now think of the Chinese lesson you are going to learn today. It is going to be as much fun and joy as whatever you were doing before. You are going to feel exactly the same joy and pleasure in learning Chinese, the same sort of fun and plesaure you got when you were learning something which gave you the same good feelings before. And learning Chinese is going to be as easy.'

Active concert

Put on the music for the active concert and begin to tell a story based on the 16 words you have chosen. This is an example of a story you can tell based on the following:

woman (女), peace (安), child (子), good (好), person/

Mind-Body Power

mankind (人), big (大), excessive (太), sky (天), sun (日), moon (月), bright (明), clear (白), understand (明白), crystal (晶), dawn (旦), written word (字).

As you tell the story, point to the character on the wall when it is mentioned in the story.

The story: *The Dawn of Chinese Civilisation*
(Remember to dramatise as much as you can by varying the tone and volume of your voice.)

> In the beginning there is Woman (女) (POINT TO WORD ON THE WALL) and she is at peace (安) with a roof over her head. Then she is with child (子). This is good (好).
> Man/mankind (人) comes along. He stretches his arms and thinks he is big (大) but when looks down and sees — AHA! WHAT DOES HE SEE !!! He sees something he has that no woman possesses and boy oh boy, does he feel smug. Now he thinks he is very big, and excessive (太) until he looks up and sees the sky (天) and realises his limitations.
> In the sky, he sees the sun (日) when he gets up, and the moon (月) when he goes to sleep. Both are bright (明). Man thinks 'The sun is so bright, just one ray is clear (白) enough. When it is bright and clear, I can understand (明白). If one ray from the sun can make everything clear, just think what three suns can do? It can make everything crystal (晶) clear!'
> And with these words from Man, the dawn (旦) of Chinese civilisation, which is the sun sitting on the horizon, emerges, for the written word (字), precious as a child in the house* comes into being.

Pseudo passive concert

Put on the Baroque largo music. Tell your friend to relax and

---

* I owe this simile to *Fun with Chinese Characters: The Straits Times Collection Vol.1*, Federal Publications, Singapore.

Teaching Others — You As Teacher

adopt the attitude that he is at a concert. Read each of the character you have put up on the wall in Chinese and its English translation eg (女) woman, (安) peace, (子) child, and so on.

The lesson ends with you telling your friend to revise the words mentally just before he falls asleep that night. He should visualise all the words he has learnt. In the morning when he wakes he should do the same thing. This is his homework.

As you can see the actual lesson takes about 30 minutes provided all the preparation has been done beforehand.

Practice

Practice is important. For this lesson, a simple practice can take the form of your friend retelling the story to you. As he does this, he should write down each character to show you.

7 New Discoveries

I am sure that now at the end of the book, you have discovered that once you have developed your mind and body power, you can achieve a greater number of life goals.

In addition, for some of you, you may have also discovered something new about yourself. You may have discovered that your physical and mental health has improved. How is that possible? Simple. In doing the exercises included in an accelerative learning or teaching programme, you body is toned, your muscles and joints are given a regular workout and your pulse rate improves.

Mentally, you are more relaxed by doing breathing and mind calming exercises. With mental relaxation comes a mind which is not as tired and jaded. You think more clearly and emotionally, you may feel better about yourself. If you feel better about yourself, it follows that you will feel better about others. In such a situation, you experience less stress with people. Less stress means that you are healthier because as everyone knows accumulated long term stress can produce illnesses which can lead to fatality such as strokes and heart attacks.

When you are not feeling as stressed, you may discover that you may smoke less, drink less and for those of you who eat when unhappy, you may even lose weight by reducing your food intake. All these improvements in your habits have a snowball effect. For instance, when you smoke less, you feel proud of yourself and the increase in self esteem may propel you to give up smoking altogether.

Just think — by learning how to speak a foreign language you end up feeling fitter both mentally and physically. By teaching a class using relaxation techniques, you end up loving yourself more as a teacher and changing your perception about the students.

New Discoveries

Some of you may have discovered that your psychic ability has improved. For instance, how many times have you known the caller before you pick up the phone during the few months of accelerative learning or teaching? This has to do with your intuitive ability as well. Our intuition is a very significant resource. It often relies on peripheral senses and the use of our right brain rather than our left. Creative visualisation techniques and Baroque music appeal to our right brain and sensitise our peripheral senses. That is why your psychic ability or intuition may improve. The more aware you are of it the greater is the possibility of you developing it. Everyone is capable of using their intuition. Some very successful businessmen and women have relied on this ability to close million dollar deals, what they often refer to as having a hunch. Intuition, hunches, having a feeling about something, psychic ability are all different ways of expressing the same thing — our unconscious speaking to us. Thus in accelerative learning programmes you cannot help but improve this dimension of your mind. Remember the unity of the conscious and the unconscious?

Our ability to heal ourselves and others can be another discovery. By using our mind power we can heal ourselves of headaches and other such conditions. This was the firm belief of Emile Coué who was a doctor practising in the French town of Nancy at the turn of the century. Thousands went to see him at his free clinic which he opened in 1910. Emile Coué fed suggestions to his patients to enable them to heal themselves. He said·

> The means employed by the healers all go back to autosuggestion, that is to say, that these methods, whatever they are, words, incantations, gestures, staging, all produce in the patient the autosuggestion of recovery.

> (Brooks:1984:36)

To be able to teach someone how to get rid of their headache or whatever psychosomatic condition they have is not much different from teaching them a language using their own mental power. I believe that is a skill that can be learnt

Mind-Body Power

as our mind power develops further. In the current state of medical science, we already have doctors practising meditative techniques on cancer patients. Perhaps the day will come when we can use our mind power as preventive measures against diseases.

The use of the mind and body potential in learning and teaching is a wonderful opening for all of us. The energy which our body and our mind generate is free. We do not have to pay a cent for it. It is there all the time and has an infinite capacity to develop and change. So why not use it? You know how now.

Appendix

BAROQUE MUSIC FOR PSEUDO PASSIVE CONCERT

ANTONIOTTO
Largo from Sonata No. 9 in C Minor (Organ and Oboe)

BACH, J.S.
First Movement Flute Sonata No. 5
Largo from Concerto in G Minor for Flute and Strings
Largo from Solo Harpsichord Concerto in G Minor
Largo from Harpsichord Concerto in F Minor
Largo from Solo Harpsichord Concerto in F Major
Aria to the Goldberg Variations
Fantasi for Organ in G Major
Fantasi in C Minor
Trio in D Minor
Prelude and Fugue in G Major
Organ Chorale in A Major

A. CORELLI
'Sarabanda' (Largo) from Concerto No. 7 in D Minor

G.F. HANDEL
Largo from 'Serse' (Organ and Trumpet)
Largo from Concerto No. 1 in F (Brass) from *Music for the Royal Fireworks*

Mind-Body Power

Largo from Concerto No. 1 in B flat Major (Woodwinds and Strings)

HERTEL
Largo from 'Partita' (Organ and Oboe)

PACHELBEL
Canon

STANLEY
Largo from Concerto No. 6 in B flat Major (Harpsichord)

G. TELEMAN, G.
Largo from Concerto for Horn and Orchestra in D Major
Largo from Sonata No. 9 in C Minor
Largo 2nd Movement from Concerto for three Oboes and three Violins in B flat Major
Largo 1st Movement from Concerto for Flute, Violin and Cello in A Major

A. VIVALDI
Largo from *Winter from the Four Seasons*
Largo from Concerto in D Minor for Viola
Largo from Concerto in D Major for Guitar and Strings
Largo from Flute Concerto No. 4 in G Major

CLASSICAL MUSIC FOR ACTIVE CONCERT

W.A. MOZART
Concerto for Violin and Orchestra No. 5 in A Major
Symphony No. 40 in G Minor
Symphony in D Major, 'Haffner' Symphony
Symphony in D Major, 'Prague' Symphony
Concerto for Piano and Orchestra No. 18 in B flat Major
Concerto for Piano and Orchestra No. 23 in A Major

J. HAYDN
Concerto No. 1 in C Major for Violin and Orchestra

Appendix

Concerto No. 2 in G Major for Violin and Orchestra
Symphony No. 101 in C Major
Symphony No. 94 in G Major

L. van BEETHOVEN
Concerto for Piano and Orchestra No. 5 in E flat Major
Concerto for Violin and Orchestra in D Major, op. 61

P. TCHAIKOVSKY
Concerto No. 1 in B Minor for Piano and Orchestra
Concerto for Violin and Orchestra in D Major, op. 35

J. BRAHMS
Concerto for Violin and Orchestra in D Major, op. 77

MOOD CREATING MUSIC

S. HALPERN
Study Suite
Eastern Peace
Starborn Suite
Spectrum Suite

References

Benson, Herbert, *Beyond the Relaxation Response*, Collins/ Fount Paperbacks, London, 1985.

Brown, Barbara, *Supermind: The Ultimate Energy*, Bantam Books, N.Y., 1983.

Coué, Emile, *Self Mastery Through Conscious Autosuggestion*, George Allen and Unwin, London, 1985.

Halpern, Steven, with Louis Savary, *Sound Health: The Music and Sound that Makes Us Whole*, Harper and Row, N.Y., 1985.

Hand, James, *Suggestopedia: The Brain and Learning*. Paper presented to the Accelerative Learning Society of Australia, La Trobe University, July 1986.

Lazarus, Anthony, *In the Minds: Power of Imagery for Personal Enrichment*, Pergamon, N.Y., 1985.

Lozanov, Georgie, *Suggestology and Outlines of Suggestopedy*, Gordon and Breach, N.Y., 1978.

Pritchard, Allyn, and Jean Taylor, *Accelerating Learning: The Use of Suggestion in the Classroom*, Academic Therapy Publications, California, 1980.

Schuster, Donald, and Charles E. Gritton, *Manual on Suggestive Accelerative Learning Techniques*, Iowa State University, 1985.

Index

active concert 23, 53, 58
anti-suggestive barriers 15
autosuggestion 8
Ayurvedic 9

Baroque largo (music) 23,
  54, 81, 84, 86, 91
Baroque music 21, 22, 23,
  60, 62, 89
barriers to learning 15
Benson, Herbert 2
biofeedback xiv, 1
Brown, Barbara xiv, 1, 2, 3,
  7

creative visualisation 40, 41,
  50, 57, 66, 85, 89
  exercises 42-48
  use of 40

desuggest 14
desuggestion 14
desuggestion-suggestion 10,
  14, 16, 19, 40
  process of 14
desuggest-suggest 66
direct nonverbal

suggestions 75
direct verbal
  suggestion(s) 71
early pleasant learning
  restimulation
  exercise 45, 55, 57, 85
encephalin 19
environmental
  suggestions 76
endorphin 19
ethical (component) 16

Freud 2

Gassner-Roberts, Sigrid xiii
goal-achievement
  exercise 42
goal setting exercise 51
goal-setting visualisation 51
Gritton, Charles xiii, 10, 70,
  71

Halpern, Steve 20, 21, 22,
  50
Hand, James 19
hyper ability 7
hypermnesia 5, 6, 11

indirect nonverbal
  suggestion(s)   75
indirect verbal suggestion   72
intuitive-affective
  (component)   16
intuitive-emotional
  barrier   15

James, William   2

Lazarus, Anthony   4
logical barrier   15
logical-critical anti-suggestive
  barrier   51
Lozanov, Georgie   xiii, xiv, 6,
  16, 21, 69
MacLaine, Shirley   3
Meares, Ansilie   4
memory improvement
  exercise   47
moral-ethical barrier   15

Pritchard   4
pseudo passive concert   23,
  54, 58

Schuster, Donald   xiii, 10,
  70, 71
Simonton, Carl   4
social psychology   8
sociology   8, 81, 82
suggestion(s)   xiii, 6, 8, 9, 11,
  12, 14, 15, 16, 17, 51, 63,
  70, 71, 76, 79, 85
  definition of   9
  history of   8
  positive   17, 51
  negative   xiii
  types of   70-76
Suggestopedia   xiii
super memory
  see hypermnesia
supermind   5

Tickner, Charles   4
Taylor   4

visualisation   42, 43, 44, 48,
  58

worry   44